Encouragement is the key word for *God-Given Dreams*. Weaving in her own storyline along with the stories of key people from the Bible, Nancy beautifully reveals that God has a plan for each one of us and that we can trust Him to fulfill it. If you're struggling with your purpose in life, encourage your spirit by reading this book, soaking in the Scripture passages, and trusting that God has His best for you.

ROCHELLE TRAUB, Our Daily Bread Ministries

As followers of Christ, we are exhorted to encourage one another to grow in the grace and knowledge of our Lord and Savior Jesus Christ (2 Peter 3:18), care for one another (Ephesians 4:32), and actively seek opportunities to show love to one another in the body of Christ (1 Peter 4:10). Nancy has spent her career in ministry as a Bible school professor doing just that, and *God-Given Dreams* is an extension of her heart to encourage believers to a more yielded, fruitful walk with our Lord! Many of our students have expressed how much they appreciate Nancy's encouragement and insight. May our Lord and Savior continue to give you success as you serve and love others.

ANTHONY HEWITT, dean of the New York School of the Bible

If you're ready to identify, confirm, and pursue your God-given dreams and do it with faith and confidence, this book is for you. The processes and biblical examples in Nancy's book will equip and empower you to make an impact on the world.

COACH REBECCA GARCIA, founder of Christian Women Entrepreneurs Network

Nancy Gavilanes specializes in making God-sized truths relevant, relatable, and applicable to our daily lives. In *God-Given Dreams*, she gives us permission (and a biblical framework) to boldly pursue the big dreams God has placed in our hearts. Though ostensibly for women, this book overflows with wisdom and encouragement that we all need to hear.

EDWARD GILBREATH, author of *Reconciliation Blues* and vice president of strategic partnerships at Christianity Today

This book is powerfully packed with steps for women to achieve their God-given dreams and assignments. Whether you are a new believer or a seasoned one, you will glean from the wisdom Nancy shares. Nancy gives you the foundation to overcome insecurities by emphasizing God's love for you and instilling confidence to know who you are in Him. This book would be a great tool for Bible-study and small groups to allow women to grow and gain the confidence to fulfill their God-given dreams.

CHRIS LUPPO, TV producer, media consultant, author, and speaker

In a world where the noise of competing values can drown out our inner calling, this book provides an encouraging oasis for you to stand firm and live your divine purpose. By weaving the author's personal journey as a Latina with profound insights from Christian practices, it invites readers of all backgrounds on a refreshing spiritual journey. It's not just about dreaming; it's about actively pursuing and courageously living your own God-given dreams.

REV. ELIZABETH TAMEZ MÉNDEZ, PhD, executive director of New Generation3, lead editor and contributing author of JUNTOSseries.com

6 WAYS TO LIVE YOUR
DIVINE PURPOSE

God-Given Dreams

NANCY GAVILANES

NavPress

A NavPress resource published in alliance
with Tyndale House Publishers

NavPress.com

A NavPress resource published in alliance with Tyndale House Publishers

NavPress and the NavPress logo are registered trademarks of NavPress, The Navigators, Colorado Springs, CO. *Tyndale* is a registered trademark of Tyndale House Ministries. Absence of ® in connection with marks of NavPress or other parties does not indicate an absence of registration of those marks.

The Team:
David Zimmerman, Publisher; Deborah Sáenz Gonzalez, Editor; Elizabeth Schroll, Copyeditor; Olivia Eldredge, Operations Manager; Sarah Susan Richardson, Designer

For information about special discounts for bulk purchases, please contact Tyndale House Publishers at csresponse@tyndale.com, or call 1-855-277-9400.

ISBN 978-1-64158-809-6

Printed in the United States of America

30	29	28	27	26	25	24
7	6	5	4	3	2	1

This book is dedicated to my loving familia, who have encouraged me and prayed for me all these years.

And also to every reader who has the courage to say yes to God's perfect will for her life.

Contents

Introduction

The Six Cs of Transformation

AS A LITTLE GIRL, I wanted to work at my favorite toy store so I could buy all the dolls I wanted. In third grade, I was fascinated with horses and dreamed of owning a horse ranch. By sixth grade, I wanted to be a pop star because I enjoyed belting out my favorite tunes.

Spoiler alert: My favorite toy store eventually closed, I'm still a city gal who doesn't own horses, and I (thankfully) outgrew my desire to be a famous singer.

Some whimsical childhood dreams are better left in the past, right?

What I didn't outgrow is my love for writing, which came as naturally to me as breathing.

I loved when my mom would read bedtime stories to me. And I still remember when she gave my older sister and me our first fancy diaries. They were so pretty that we each immediately put a prized pink satin sticker on our covers. I was eight years old, and it felt normal to jot down little notes about my ordinary days.

When I was in fifth grade, my sister and I would spend hours making magazines out of loose-leaf paper. We joyfully wrote all the articles, drew all the pictures, and bound the pages together with tape or staples. I still have the six issues I created. My sister was my only reader.

I thought everyone enjoyed writing.

As a teen, my writing dreams were to work at a magazine and to go to the Olympics as a reporter.

I'm not sure how I even had the audacity to form such big aspirations at that age. I was just a young writer who enjoyed reading magazines and admired Olympians. I didn't know any reporters or elite athletes. And I had no idea how I could ever reach those goals, which seemed as outrageous as going to the moon.

Looking back at my life, I now see that writing was a gift from God. And while I had plans for my future, God had His own divine plans.

I'm a Latina from New York and the daughter of two hardworking and loving parents who immigrated from Central and South America as young adults. My mother and late father were the first in their large families to leave their respective home countries on planes bound for the United States. Unknowingly, they arrived in the Big

Apple just months apart from each other. They came in search of better opportunities, and they did so at a time when there were few Latinos in New York. They met soon after arriving, married, and later had my sister and me. I saw my parents struggle and succeed at attaining their American dreams, and that has left a lasting impression on me.

Now I can see that I come from a family of dreamers and doers.

When you're the daughter of immigrants, or an immigrant yourself, you tend to have that extra drive (or ganas) to want to succeed and make your parents and extended family proud.

So I worked hard to achieve my personal goals. I graduated with a master's degree in journalism from New York University and started to experience success in my career. I was seeing my dreams come true but had drifted far from God.

When I finally dedicated my life to God, the trajectory of my life changed. Instead of pursuing my goals, I started pursuing God and dreaming with Him.

That's made all the difference in my life.

God called me out of a successful journalism career to speak and write about Him. The process hasn't been easy, and I haven't had a huge cheering squad in my corner. But after many years of prayer, preparation, and experience,

I'm now an author, speaker, Christian life coach, Bible school instructor, podcaster, and evangelist.

I've been blessed to see God's miraculous fingerprints on six continents.

I've had the honor of speaking to various groups, including Christians working at the United Nations, chapel attendees at a Christian college, and wonderful women living at a shelter. I've been a small-group leader, a Bible-class facilitator, a short-term missionary in five countries, a volunteer chaplain, an evangelistic-outreach leader, and a counselor and coach to friends and family.

A big part of my calling is to encourage and empower faithful and fabulous women of God like you!

DARE TO DREAM WITH GOD

Throughout my years of ministry, I've had the privilege and honor of ministering to countless precious women. The women I've met may vary in age, race, ethnicity, and background, but many share a similar struggle of not having the courage, confidence, or clarity to pursue their God-given dreams.

It's as if they're afraid to dream big or are waiting for permission to proceed.

Many feel their dreams are only daydreams. Their goals seem unattainable or impossible.

There are many reasons why some women stop short of taking steps toward their dreams.

Many grew up feeling pressured to fit a certain role or stereotype. Others lack the opportunities or resources to move forward. Some were raised in abusive households or other toxic environments that left them feeling insecure and afraid. Others just haven't had access to mentors or role models who could give them a glimpse of what it's like to work in a certain career or serve in a certain capacity. They lack someone who can remind them of their extreme worth, nurture their gifts, and coach them along their path.

These women doubt they have what it takes. They feel stuck because they don't know how to get started. They're worried about what others might think or say. Some feel disqualified because of their rocky start in life, their nationality or accent, or their current circumstances.

Can you relate?

Maybe you're there now.

If you've ever wondered whether God loves you or has a plan for your life, or if you've ever questioned if God could use you to make a difference in this world, this book is for you.

If you've ever felt underestimated, misunderstood, or even marginalized, this book is for you.

If you've felt as though your dreams don't matter or are too far-fetched, this book is for you.

If you're feeling stuck and unsure about how to start living your God-given dreams, this book is for you.

If you're ready to take prayerful and bold steps toward your God-given purpose, this book is for you.

GOD'S BELOVED DREAMER

What dreams has God placed in your heart?

What stirs your soul and keeps you up at night?

What breakthrough have you been waiting and longing for?

How would your life—and the lives of those you seek to help—change if you were living your God-given dreams?

What's holding you back from taking steps toward your God-given dreams?

I know how frustrating it can be to try to figure out what God's calling you to do, how confusing it can be to try to map out what steps to take, and how daunting it can feel when it seems like the odds are stacked against you.

It can feel discouraging, disappointing, and downright disheartening. It can even make you question whether you somehow misheard God.

Thankfully, I also know the joy of being at the center

of God's will and have experienced the blessings that come with answering God's call.

My prayer is that you will also know the joy of being God's beloved dreamer and will be able to flourish in all that God is calling you to do.

God already knows what's on the other side of our yes!

YOUR GOD-GIVEN DREAMS MATTER

In this book I'll be sharing some of the Bible verses, Bible heroines (who I call "Bible beauties"), and Bible-based principles that have helped me on my journey. May you be inspired, challenged, and empowered to dare to live your God-given dreams and purpose.

God has made you for such a time as this.

You matter. Your God-given dreams matter.

The world needs you to take your place, wherever God is calling you. People need to hear your voice. They need you to be that salt and light and that woman of God who will be His hands and feet to express His love to those near and far.

You are the answer to someone's prayers. Will you let God use you as He sees fit?

Will you say yes to God's call on your life?

I love seeing women walk in a way worthy of their calling.

There's a time to dream, and then there's a time to do!

I'm looking forward to spurring you on in your journey to your breakthrough.

Are you ready to do some prayerful soul searching to discover how God has designed you?

WHO DO YOU SEE WHEN YOU LOOK IN THE MIRROR?

Do you like who you see when you look in the mirror?

Can you see past her seeming imperfections? Can you accept her—flaws and all?

Can you see past the labels placed on her by society, her cultural heritage, her leaders, or her family members?

And who are you behind your smile? Who are you when no one is looking?

Do you like the woman you've become? Can you love her despite her past? Can you look beyond her outward appearance and résumé, or her lack of experience?

Or do you get hung up on her scars and blemishes, both visible and internal? Do you judge her by her past sins, failures, and poor choices, or even her present circumstances?

Do you feel unlovely, unlovable, unworthy, or unqualified? Are you filled with doubt, insecurity, or fear? Do you question whether you have what it takes to make a difference in the world?

Are you afraid you're all alone, not enough, unwanted, or anonymous?

Ever wish you could trade places with the gal who seems to have it all together on social media or TV, at the office, or in the classroom?

Do you struggle to fit in or to feel like you belong? Do you know who you are? Do you know your real worth?

I'm here to remind you that God loves you beyond measure. You are God's unique masterpiece! God is with you. You are not alone.

God sees you and hears you. God is closer than you think. God is closer than your next breath. God is working out His perfect plan for you.

Don't listen to what the critics, the cynics, the haters, or even society says about you.

You are beloved, blessed, and beautiful.

God loves you more than you'll ever know!

DISCOVERING THE SIX Cs OF TRANSFORMATION

In this book, we'll go on a journey to discover, embrace, and celebrate who we are in Christ using the Six Cs of Transformation. I prayerfully created this framework for my coaching clients and Bible school students to help them go from feeling frustrated to fruitful, frazzled to focused, and fearful to fierce.

Let's rejoice even now that we are

- *created* by almighty God;
- *called* to honor God;
- *chosen* to bear fruit;
- *conformed* to the image of Christ;
- *clothed* with purpose; and
- *commissioned* to shine and soar.

My prayer is that each chapter of this book will flood you with the love of God. May you be captivated and enthralled, and may your heart and soul be stirred!

Once we know who we are in Christ, we're unstoppable.

God sees us, flaws and all, and loves us!

God's love for us is extravagant. He longs to lavish His love on us.

We are God's beloved. God is doing a beautiful work in us.

When God sees you, He sees Jesus.

Jesus has redeemed you.

You are precious in His sight.

Look up.

Stand tall.

Stand strong.

You are a blood-bought daughter of the living God.

Be kind to the woman smiling at you in the mirror. She is precious and dearly loved.

You are the one who captivates God's heart.

Walk in God's love. Bask in God's love.

Receive it. Remain in it. Reflect it. Rejoice in it.

Hold fast to what God says about you, and dare to live your God-given dreams!

CHAPTER 1

Created by Almighty God

You created my inmost being; you knit me together in my mother's womb. I praise you because I am fearfully and wonderfully made; your works are wonderful, I know that full well. My frame was not hidden from you when I was made in the secret place, when I was woven together in the depths of the earth. Your eyes saw my unformed body; all the days ordained for me were written in your book before one of them came to be.

PSALM 139:13-16

"THIS IS FOR YOU TO write things down," my mom said as she handed my older sister and me our new diaries. I was eight years old, and I was enthralled by the pretty notebook with pink pages and hearts all over the cover. It was from the fancy store where everything was covered in pastel colors and cute cartoon characters.

I didn't know what I'd write in this special book, but I couldn't wait to get started. First came placing a satin sticker on the cover, and next came the writing.

I wrote about ordinary things like playing with my sister or pets or cousins and going to the dentist. I also wrote simple prayers or hopes for upcoming events.

Private and introverted me welcomed having a space where I could jot down whatever random thoughts or experiences I was having. I thought everyone wrote about their daily lives.

I continued to journal my thoughts in notebook after notebook. Writing became second nature to me.

My parents made sure I had scores of books to read and plenty of paper and pens on hand. They encouraged me to hone my writing skills, and they delighted in celebrating even my earliest published articles in high school, college, and local newspapers.

My dear late dad, who was from Ecuador, and my precious mom, who is from Central America, both ran successful small businesses in New York. They modeled and instilled in my sister and me the value of working hard to achieve your goals.

My parents immigrated to New York at a time when speaking Spanish was extremely frowned upon in the neighborhood. They had learned English in their respective home countries and continued studying and practicing English once they were in the United States. While I grew up in a bilingual home, English is my dominant language. It's the language I used when speaking to my sister and to my school friends. English was the language my family tended to use outside the home—to blend in, I guess, and not draw attention to ourselves.

Spanish was reserved for the adults. They used it mostly inside our home and especially when familia from abroad came to visit. Spanish always felt like a second language to me. It always felt more natural to express myself in English.

Funny enough, I only recently learned the reason I ended up in a bilingual kindergarten class: The school was overcrowded. When my parents found out I was in a bilingual class, they thought it was good for me to be exposed to both languages. At the time I didn't realize there was anything different about my class, but now I see it helped prepare me for my Spanglish world.

Even as adults, my dad and I spoke mainly in English, whether indoors or outdoors. That was our heart language with each other. My mom and I have a unique way of communicating. She speaks to me mainly in Spanish, and I respond mainly in English. Over the years, people in stores have been baffled to hear us speaking to each other in different languages.

I'm grateful that I'm fluent enough in Spanish to draw on it as needed. I know that being Latina means more than just how well I speak español or how I look or sound.

As a native New Yorker, I grew up surrounded by vibrant Hispanic culture as well as a beautiful mosaic of other cultures. As diverse as my city was, I wasn't usually surrounded by many other Latina or Latino writers.

Many of my Latina/o peers didn't know what to do with me.

"You're not Spanish, you just look it," some acquaintances would say. I guess my interests and experiences were different from those around me. As a teen and young adult, I did struggle with embracing my Latina roots.

But I'm glad that didn't stop me from putting pen to paper.

In my sophomore year of high school, I joined the school's newspaper. The English teacher who oversaw the newspaper was a tough editor, but she saw potential in me and my writing. She helped affirm that I was a good writer. I reluctantly became the editor-in-chief of the paper in my senior year.

When the time came to choose a college major, journalism seemed like the best fit. While I did have a professor in a Latin American studies class who introduced me to books by Latina authors, I was the only Latina student in my journalism classes. It didn't really bother me, but I noticed it. I'm glad my professors treated me fairly. I did feel like the odd one out during our required internship, though, when journalism majors moved to another city for six months to write for a local paper. I was the only Latina in our small group. Our editor enjoyed giving us nicknames, and he chose to call me "Sally Sombrero." That irked me, but I didn't say anything.

Whether I was writing for my college newspaper or interning at weekly papers, I enjoyed telling stories that gave a voice to the voiceless or informed readers about issues happening on campus or in the community.

I had the great honor of being the second person in mi familia to graduate from college.

After graduation, I worked at a prestigious newspaper as a news clerk and then started writing articles and book reviews for them. At my dad's urging, I went to graduate school and got a master's degree in journalism from New York University. I then worked at a women's magazine in Times Square. All my journalism dreams were coming true.

Unfortunately, as my writing career soared, my walk with God suffered. I thought I had outgrown God, and I tried to put Him on a shelf.

I was bored with church and tired of religion, and I didn't read my Bible, which I had only used back in school when I had religion-class homework. None of my friends were going to church anymore, so I thought this was all normal.

I was making my plans and asking God to bless them.

Big mistake.

One of my biggest career aspirations was to attend the Olympics as a reporter. I was ecstatic when I received the opportunity to travel to the Summer Games in Sydney, Australia, as a reporter and a spectator!

I had a lovely time there, but something wasn't right. I had reached my goals and had gotten myself as far as I could, but I still wasn't satisfied.

My purpose in Sydney was to chase down athletes. God's purpose was to send the Holy Spirit to chase *me* down.

During my last full day there, I was by myself in Olympic Park, crying and still feeling empty.

I started to think about all that God had allowed me to accomplish in such a short amount of time, even though I had been rebelling against Him. I felt overwhelmed by God's amazing love and grace and mercy. I knew I didn't deserve any of these blessings.

All my mom's and sister's prayers from over the years must've finally kicked in.

I realized I needed to turn to God.

Right there in Olympic Park (without a pastor or evangelist with me), I surrendered my life to God and dedicated myself to serving Him. I started to realize that God had created me with great love. Almighty God has a plan for my life. And God has a plan for your life too.

CREATED WITH EXTRAVAGANT LOVE

If you've ever felt invisible, inadequate, or insecure, you're not alone. Many people struggle to feel valuable and significant.

Many times, this stems from having a strained relationship with a parent or from having toxic people around us, especially during childhood. It could be compounded by harsh words or abusive actions from a spouse, a boss, or others.

Society, peers, and circumstances may also make us think we're not enough or we don't have what it takes. We need to shatter those lies. Thoughts that you'll never amount to anything, or you're no good, or God could never love you are lies from the pit of hell. The enemy wants to fool us into thinking we're unloved, unworthy, or unwanted. He wants to steal, kill, and destroy our lives and rob us of our identity.

But the enemy is a liar and defeated!

The first truth in the Six Cs of Transformation is that God created us with extravagant love. Almighty God, the Creator of heaven and earth—the One who made the sun, moon, and stars and created the splendid array of gorgeous flowers, spectacular sunrises and sunsets, and the breathtaking sea—delighted in creating each one of us.

In one of the very first verses in the Bible, we read: "God created mankind in his own image, in the image of God he created them; male and female he created them" (Genesis 1:27).

Even King David marveled at knowing we're God's creation. In Psalm 8 he wrote:

When I consider your heavens,
    the work of your fingers,
the moon and the stars,
    which you have set in place,
what is mankind that you are mindful
      of them,
    human beings that you care for them?

PSALM 8:3-4

The next time you see an exquisite sunset, sea, or flower, remember how lovely you are in God's sight! You were created to worship Him. You were created to bring Him glory.

God didn't make any mistakes when He created you.

He knew exactly where and when you would be born. He knew the shape of your nose and eyes, the color of your skin, your height, and even the funny way you laugh. God designed you as He saw fit.

FEARFULLY AND WONDERFULLY MADE

Psalm 139 is one of my favorite psalms because it describes how God fashioned and formed us with great love and attention:

You created my inmost being;
    you knit me together in my mother's womb.

I praise you because I am fearfully and
    wonderfully made;
  your works are wonderful,
  I know that full well.
My frame was not hidden from you
  when I was made in the secret place,
  when I was woven together in the depths
    of the earth.
Your eyes saw my unformed body;
  all the days ordained for me were written in
    your book
  before one of them came to be.
How precious to me are your thoughts, God!
  How vast is the sum of them!
Were I to count them,
  they would outnumber the grains of sand—
  when I awake, I am still with you.

PSALM 139:13-18

We're not anonymous or random to God. God knows us by name and knows our thoughts and every hair on our heads.

When I was alone in Australia, I may have been anonymous to the people all around me, but God saw me and knew everything about me. He knew I'd be at the park that afternoon. He didn't scold or punish me.

He just loved me. That meant the world to me and reminded me that I couldn't outrun God's love, even when I was on the other side of the globe. God truly is everywhere.

God knew us before we were in our mothers' wombs and has a plan for every one of our days. *We are fearfully and wonderfully made in God's image.* Let that truth sink in.

The woman who stares back at you in the mirror each morning is dearly loved by God and is His masterpiece. This fact should silence any lies you may have believed. Let it change the way you see yourself.

God does wonderful works, and you are one of them! We are the apple of God's eye, engraved on the palms of His hands. We are God's beloved, and we are precious and honored.

GOD'S BELOVED DAUGHTER

Even with our quirks, imperfections, messy pasts, or insecurities, we are precious to God.

In Matthew 3:17, God declares His love for His Son, Jesus: "A voice from heaven said, 'This is my Son, whom I love; with him I am well pleased.'"

In some Bible translations, God calls Jesus His "beloved Son." God *deeply* loves His Son, Jesus, and the Father and Son are one. If you consider how much God loves Jesus, John 15:9 will blow your mind and warm your heart. Listen to what Jesus tells His disciples:

"As the Father has loved me, so have I loved you. Now remain in my love."

Did you catch that? Jesus loves His disciples (including you and me) as God loves Him. It's almost too incredible to believe, but let that truth reach the deepest part of your heart. *Jesus loves you as the Father loves Him.*

During my "lost years," when I was living as I pleased and asking God to bless my plans, I felt far from Him. Though I loved God, I felt like there was a wall between us. I felt like God was mad at me for my rebellious ways, and I wondered if He still loved me.

That wall was smashed when I realized that I could be reconciled to my heavenly Father through Jesus, as it says throughout the Bible (in 1 Timothy 2:5-6, for example). Even when I felt far from God, God had never left me.

God has precious thoughts toward us. He knew us before we were in our mothers' wombs. He loved us before we could love Him. He loved us even when we were His enemies and rebelling against Him. We can't do anything to earn His love. Romans 5:8 states: "God demonstrates his own love for us in this: While we were still sinners, Christ died for us."

God loves us even though He knows our past, present, and future sins.

When we receive Jesus as our Lord and Savior, He comes to live inside us, as we read in Colossians 1:27: "To them God has chosen to make known among the Gentiles the glorious riches of this mystery, which is Christ in you, the hope of glory."

We also become God's beloved children, as the apostle Paul wrote in Galatians 3:26-28:

> In Christ Jesus you are all children of God through faith, for all of you who were baptized into Christ have clothed yourselves with Christ. There is neither Jew nor Gentile, neither slave nor free, nor is there male and female, for you are all one in Christ Jesus.

God isn't some distant being floating around in the universe. He is our heavenly Father, according to Romans 8:14-17:

> Those who are led by the Spirit of God are the children of God. The Spirit you received does not make you slaves, so that you live in fear again; rather, the Spirit you received brought about your adoption to sonship. And by him we cry, "*Abba,* Father." The Spirit himself testifies with our spirit

that we are God's children. Now if we are children, then we are heirs—heirs of God and co-heirs with Christ, if indeed we share in his sufferings in order that we may also share in his glory.

May we never take for granted that we, like a child speaking to her daddy, can call God "*Abba*, Father."

GLEANING INSIGHT FROM A BIBLE BEAUTY

Ruth is a beautiful example of what it looks like to be created with extravagant love by God.

When we first meet Ruth, we learn she is a young widow. She had been married to a Hebrew man named Mahlon. Ruth was a Moabite. Her people were longtime rivals of the Israelites.

Mahlon and his family had moved to Moab during a severe famine in Bethlehem. While in Moab, Mahlon died, and so did his father and brother. Ruth's elderly mother-in-law, Naomi, was devastated and heartbroken, and she made plans to return to Bethlehem since the famine was over.

What was Ruth to do?

Ruth could've stayed in Moab with her parents and restarted her life there. Naomi even urged her several times to stay. But Ruth made a defining decision that changed the course of her life. Ruth chose to leave Moab and go with Naomi to Bethlehem. Ruth chose to forsake her people's gods to follow the God of Israel.

Ruth had no idea what lay in store for her. She emigrated to a new land. As a foreigner and a widow, she was among the most vulnerable in society.

It looked like Ruth was headed for a life of poverty and suffering. She may have felt unqualified, unwanted, and unfit for any other kind of life.

But God had created Ruth with extravagant love.

God knew Ruth was a Moabite. He wasn't surprised by her background. And God hadn't abandoned Ruth or Naomi.

Ruth put her trust in God, and God came through for her.

God provided food and work for Ruth. And God led Ruth to glean in a field belonging to Boaz, a kinsman redeemer (a relative close enough to buy the land from Naomi's family to keep it in their family line). Boaz and Ruth soon married and had a son named Obed. Obed was the father of Jesse, who was the father of King David.

Ruth, a hardworking immigrant who humbly served her family and others, is King David's great-grandmother and one of Jesus' ancestors. She is one of only five women mentioned in Jesus' genealogy (see Matthew 1:5) and one of only two women to have a book of the Bible named after her.

God truly worked all things together for Ruth's good.

Almighty God *created* Ruth with extravagant love.

God *called* Ruth to honor Him.

God *chose* Ruth to bear fruit.

God *conformed* Ruth to the image of Christ.

God *clothed* Ruth with purpose.

God *commissioned* Ruth to shine and soar for Him.

BEING ROOTED AND GROUNDED IN GOD'S LOVE

Before we can dare to live our God-given dreams, it's essential that we become rooted and grounded in God's extravagant and everlasting love.

Sometimes our past hurts or current disappointments prevent us from believing that God loves us. Or maybe you grew up thinking God was the mean "Man Upstairs" who was always mad at you and waiting for you to make mistakes.

Beloved, may you keep your heart open and ready to receive all the love and goodness and kindness and mercy God wants to shower on you. May you remain in God's love today and always.

God is the definition of love, as the apostle John stated in 1 John 4:16-17:

God is love. Whoever lives in love lives in God, and God in them. This is how love is made complete

among us so that we will have confidence on the
day of judgment: In this world we are like Jesus.

If we truly accepted how much God loves us, it
wouldn't matter what other people thought about us. We
would walk with confidence, clarity, and courage because
our identity would be wrapped in Christ.

How would your life change if you lived as the beloved
child of God that you are?

How much more secure and significant would you
feel if you remembered that God doesn't stop loving you?

Nothing can separate us from God's love. Romans
8:38-39 is a wonderful passage to memorize and meditate
on: "I am convinced that neither death nor life, neither
angels nor demons, neither the present nor the future, nor
any powers, neither height nor depth, nor anything else
in all creation, will be able to separate us from the love of
God that is in Christ Jesus our Lord."

What a beautiful truth: We are dearly and eternally
loved by God! The apostle Paul prayed that the Ephesians
would be able to grasp the magnitude of God's extravagant love. This prayer is my prayer for us as well:

For this reason I kneel before the Father, from
whom every family in heaven and on earth
derives its name. I pray that out of his glorious

riches he may strengthen you with power through his Spirit in your inner being, so that Christ may dwell in your hearts through faith. And I pray that you, being rooted and established in love, may have power, together with all the Lord's holy people, to grasp how wide and long and high and deep is the love of Christ, and to know this love that surpasses knowledge—that you may be filled to the measure of all the fullness of God.

EPHESIANS 3:14-19

Being rooted and grounded in Christ's love is the firm foundation we need to flourish in all areas of our lives.

REFLECTING ON BEING CREATED TO LOVE GOD AND OTHERS

As we meditate on God's goodness and receive His extravagant love, our natural response will be to lavish Him with love.

We love because he first loved us.

1 JOHN 4:19

If you want a clearer picture of God the Father, look at the life, ministry, and character of His Son, Jesus. Jesus is the image of the invisible God.

Jesus is also the Good Shepherd. A friend who sticks closer than a brother. The Way, the Truth, and the Life. The Bread of Life. The Lamb of God. Immanuel, which means "God with Us." The Wonderful Counselor, Mighty God, Everlasting Father, and Prince of Peace. The Resurrection and the Life.

Once you receive God's amazing and extravagant love, you'll be able to serve as an expression of His love to others, who also need a taste of God's infinite love for them.

Empowered by God's love, we're able to love our neighbors and make a difference in our communities and beyond.

Is your heart being stirred?

You were created with a divine purpose. Are you ready to take the next step toward living your God-given dreams?

REFLECTION QUESTIONS

I hope these questions will help stir your heart. You can use them as journal prompts or as discussion questions with your small group.

1. Are you feeling God's unconditional love for you? If so, stop and soak it in, and then write a prayer thanking God for His extravagant love.

2. Has something been hindering you from receiving and reveling in God's love for you? If so, ask God to expose the lies you've been believing and to help you replace those lies with His truth.

3. How does Ruth's story inspire you and demonstrate that almighty God creates us with extravagant love?

4. Have you received Jesus as your Lord and Savior? If so, describe that glorious day. If not, what's stopping you?

5. How would your life change if you truly received and remained in God's extravagant love for you? Would you feel ready to dare to live your God-given dreams?

6. What is one key takeaway or insight you learned from this chapter?

7. What's one faith step you can prayerfully commit to taking this week to get closer to living your God-given dreams?

ACTION STEP

Write a letter to yourself reminding you just how beloved, blessed, and beautiful you are to God. Read it out loud to yourself while facing a mirror. Keep the letter handy so you can read it whenever you need a sweet reminder that God loves you.

PRAYER AND PRAISE

Lord, thank You for Your extravagant love, grace, and mercy. Thank You that I am fearfully and wonderfully made by You. Forgive me for doubting Your love or concern for me. Help me receive Your unmerited, unlimited, and unconditional love for me. Today, I'm praising You and praying for . . .

CHAPTER 2

Called to Honor God

We are God's handiwork, created in Christ Jesus to do good works,
which God prepared in advance for us to do.

EPHESIANS 2:10

I STILL REMEMBER THE DAY I felt God calling me to lay down my journalism career. I was at my first retreat as an adult with my new Christian friends. During a break, I was reading my Bible by a pond, and I felt the Lord asking me to step away from my life as a journalist and follow Him.

This came as a shock to me. Journalism was all I knew. I was obsessed with elite sports and hooked on writing about elite athletes. Though I had slowly been growing disillusioned with the field, I didn't think I was ready to walk away from it completely.

I had just gotten a job offer to help bring the Olympics

to my hometown. That would've been a dream job for me before this retreat, but something changed that weekend. I knew this part of my life and career was coming to an end.

It was as if God was saying, "I hope you enjoyed all that I allowed you to experience, because I have work for you to do now."

God was showing me that my career ambitions and obsession with sports had become idols.

As a teen, I was consumed with certain sports. I went from being a fan to taking skating and gymnastics lessons for three years so I could experience these sports in a deeper way. I would ask my parents to take me to skating or gymnastics events near and far. I would read all the magazines and spend hours watching and rewatching competitions on TV because I didn't want to miss a moment.

I now realize I was using sports as a way of escape, just as some teens get lost in video games or other interests. When I was engrossed in the beauty and pageantry and excitement of elite sports, I didn't have to think about my parents' bitter divorce or any other problems in my life.

As a reporter, I got to meet many elite athletes, and I was able to interview and photograph them for various publications. As thrilling as that was, I still felt empty.

I was always striving to meet the next athlete or go to the next event.

Although part of the reason I became a journalist was to tell the stories that others weren't telling, it eventually became more of a game to see where my byline would appear next and what big interview I could score next. In Sydney, I felt God point out that I knew more about famous athletes than about His promises for me in the Bible. And it must've been the Holy Spirit who pointed out that I would fly to the other side of the world for a sporting competition and wake up early on a Sunday morning to watch koalas being fed at the zoo, but back home I couldn't go a few blocks to church.

I may have been trying to write my life story, but God had a plot twist for me.

Over the years I've learned that how we respond in these sacred moments makes all the difference in the world.

When we feel God calling and inviting us to colabor with Him, we shouldn't take it lightly.

God longs for us to say yes!

As we mature in our faith and our relationship with God, we can continue to say yes when we feel God prompting us to do certain things.

A seemingly small and insignificant yes can lead to a much bigger yes down the road.

God doesn't call everyone to leave their jobs. There was nothing wrong with my enjoying sports or choosing journalism as a career path. What I learned is that our careers or hobbies shouldn't consume us, and that they shouldn't be the center of our identity.

Our life and worth and value should center on our identity in Christ.

Have you felt God trying to woo you and get your attention? God knows how to whisper to our hearts and speak to us even in the midnight hours. Many times, people are afraid that God will ask them to do something they won't like. We need to remember how much God loves us, and that He has our best interests at heart, always.

I'm grateful that God met me that day in Sydney and that He later called me out of journalism.

I may not have known what lay ahead, but by faith I said yes to His call.

Instead of rebelling and running away from God, I ran toward Him.

CALLED TO HONOR GOD

The second truth in the Six Cs of Transformation is that God has called us to honor Him.

Our lives are not our own. Almighty God, our Creator,

has called us to worship Him and bring glory to His name through our lives.

As Christians, we're called to walk by faith and to love and serve and pray for one another. We're called to follow Jesus, obey His teachings, pray without ceasing, and love our neighbors, just to name a few of the instructions found in Scripture.

Living for Christ is our main calling, but God also has a one-of-a-kind plan for every one of His children. There's a unique call on your life.

God created you with extravagant love and called you to honor Him. As God's love overflows in you, you'll find yourself wanting to serve and honor Him with your life.

God loves us, and He demonstrated His love with action by sending Jesus to redeem us. We are to demonstrate our love and faith in God with action, for the Bible says faith without works is dead.

But we need to get our priorities right. We need to seek God's presence in our lives more than we seek His presents or blessings.

As we learned in chapter 1, we need to be rooted and grounded in God's love. Only then can we genuinely pour out that love on others and serve them wholeheartedly.

We need to spend time with Jesus.

The more time we spend reading the Bible, praying,

and worshiping, the more our hearts will align with God's heart.

Our hearts are cleansed and healed as we spend time with Jesus, the Lover of our souls and Healer of our hearts. We'll talk more about that in chapter 4.

In this chapter, we're taking a closer look at staying attuned to God's call on our lives. As you read, pray. Ask God to show you the divine call He's placed on your life and the unique Kingdom assignments He is preparing you to accomplish to honor Him.

HEARING GOD'S CALL

The next step to daring to live your God-given dreams is discovering the unique call God has placed on you, His beloved, blessed, and beautiful daughter. Let's start by looking at how God called a few well-known Bible figures.

I find God's words to the prophet Jeremiah so inspiring:

> "Before I formed you in the womb I knew you,
>   before you were born I set you apart;
>   I appointed you as a prophet to the nations."
>
> JEREMIAH 1:5

I love how God set apart Jeremiah for His purposes before the prophet was even born. That means Jeremiah couldn't do anything to deserve that call and that no one could reverse God's sovereign decision.

Since God doesn't show favoritism, His calling comes before we could ever earn or deserve it. God calls us as He sees fit.

How astounding it is to know our Everlasting God has been preparing us for our Kingdom assignments since before we were even born.

When the prophet Samuel was just a boy, he heard someone calling his name during the night. He thought it was Eli, the high priest, so he ran to his mentor. But after this had happened three times, Eli realized the Lord was calling Samuel. Eli told the boy to go back to bed in case God called again, and he told him what to say. Here's the beautiful way the boy responded to God's call:

> The Lord came and stood there, calling as at the
> other times, "Samuel! Samuel!"
>
> Then Samuel said, "Speak, for your servant is
> listening."
>
> 1 SAMUEL 3:10

Young Samuel heard God's call and obeyed. He grew up to become one of Israel's greatest prophets, and he anointed King Saul and King David.

What if Samuel had rejected God's call on his life?

What if *we* reject God's call on our lives?

Sometimes God's call can seem foolish. Just ask Noah.

God called Noah to build a boat . . . on dry land.

Did Noah try to negotiate with God or ignore His mandate?

Nope.

God knew He could trust Noah with this assignment, as we read in Genesis:

> Noah did everything just as God commanded him.
>
> GENESIS 6:22

God trusts us with all that He's called us to do. He will give us the courage and confidence we need to fulfill His call on our lives.

When we consider how God called Jeremiah, Samuel, and Noah, we can be inspired as we listen for God to call us to draw closer to Him and as we discern His unique call on our lives.

We may feel scared or intimidated as we wonder what God might ask us to do, but let's remain open to hearing what God wants to say to us.

CALLED TO SAY YES TO GOD

Not everyone rejoices when they hear God calling them. Let's look at a few Bible characters who weren't so eager to answer God's call on their lives. We can learn from their experiences as well.

Moses must've been filled with fear when God told him to order Pharaoh to let His people go.

In Exodus 4:10-12, we read Moses' attempt at changing God's mind:

> Moses said to the LORD, "Pardon your servant, Lord. I have never been eloquent, neither in the past nor since you have spoken to your servant. I am slow of speech and tongue."
>
> The LORD said to him, "Who gave human beings their mouths? Who makes them deaf or mute? Who gives them sight or makes them blind? Is it not I, the LORD? Now go; I will help you speak and will teach you what to say."

Moses still wasn't convinced he was the right person for the job: "But Moses said, 'Pardon your servant, Lord. Please send someone else'" (Exodus 4:13).

God didn't seem impressed by Moses' excuses. He had created Moses. He knew all about Moses' insecurities. He had appointed Moses for this assignment.

God gave Moses signs, sent his brother, Aaron, as backup, and promised to be with him. But He didn't let Moses off the hook.

God also wasn't fazed by Gideon's excuses.

Gideon was hiding from the Midianites when God called him:

> The angel of the LORD came and sat down under the oak in Ophrah that belonged to Joash the Abiezrite, where his son Gideon was threshing wheat in a winepress to keep it from the Midianites. When the angel of the LORD appeared to Gideon, he said, "The LORD is with you, mighty warrior."
>
> "Pardon me, my lord," Gideon replied, "but if the LORD is with us, why has all this happened to us? Where are all his wonders that our ancestors told us about when they said, 'Did not the LORD bring us up out of Egypt?' But now the LORD has abandoned us and given us into the hand of Midian."
>
> The LORD turned to him and said, "Go in the strength you have and save Israel out of Midian's hand. Am I not sending you?"
>
> "Pardon me, my lord," Gideon replied, "but how can I save Israel? My clan is the weakest in Manasseh, and I am the least in my family."

The Lord answered, "I will be with you, and you will strike down all the Midianites, leaving none alive."

JUDGES 6:11-16

God was calling Gideon to the Kingdom tasks He had ordained for him. Gideon was too busy having a pity party. His people had been oppressed by the Midianites for seven years. Gideon didn't feel qualified to help free them.

God knew Gideon was genuinely afraid and needed much reassurance, so God patiently waited as Gideon prepared his offering, and He went along with Gideon's infamous fleece test that we read about in Judges 6:36-40:

Gideon said to God, "If you will save Israel by my hand as you have promised—look, I will place a wool fleece on the threshing floor. If there is dew only on the fleece and all the ground is dry, then I will know that you will save Israel by my hand, as you said." And that is what happened. Gideon rose early the next day; he squeezed the fleece and wrung out the dew— a bowlful of water.

Then Gideon said to God, "Do not be angry with me. Let me make just one more request.

Allow me one more test with the fleece, but this time make the fleece dry and let the ground be covered with dew." That night God did so. Only the fleece was dry; all the ground was covered with dew.

We probably would've given up on Gideon for stalling so much and asking for so many signs, but God didn't give up on Gideon.

God called Gideon and gave him the courage and strength and wisdom he needed to accomplish His mission for him.

Note that Moses and Gideon both needed an extra dose of encouragement to live out the respective calls on their lives.

Moses had tried to liberate God's people in his early years, but he got himself into big trouble (see Exodus 2:11-15).

Gideon likely never would've mustered up the courage to defeat his oppressors on his own.

The same is true for us: We need God's help to live His purposes for our lives.

We're not meant to accomplish God's will without Him.

Sometimes when God called people in the Bible, their reaction was to feel unworthy. That was especially true with the prophet Isaiah, who received his call during a vision of God seated on His throne:

> "Woe to me!" I cried. "I am ruined! For I am a man of unclean lips, and I live among a people of unclean lips, and my eyes have seen the King, the LORD Almighty."
>
> Then one of the seraphim flew to me with a live coal in his hand, which he had taken with tongs from the altar. With it he touched my mouth and said, "See, this has touched your lips; your guilt is taken away and your sin atoned for."
>
> Then I heard the voice of the Lord saying, "Whom shall I send? And who will go for us?"
>
> And I said, "Here am I. Send me!"
>
> ISAIAH 6:5-8

In this sacred moment, God brought Isaiah from feeling insecure and disqualified to being fully surrendered and qualified. How lovely this is to see!

The apostle Peter also struggled when Jesus called him, as Luke 5:8-11 records:

> When Simon Peter saw this, he fell at Jesus' knees and said, "Go away from me, Lord; I am

a sinful man!" For he and all his companions were astonished at the catch of fish they had taken, and so were James and John, the sons of Zebedee, Simon's partners.

Then Jesus said to Simon, "Don't be afraid; from now on you will fish for people." So they pulled their boats up on shore, left everything and followed him.

How amazing that Jesus' reassuring words helped Peter go from feeling ashamed and unworthy to casting everything aside to follow Him.

God is calling us, too.

Let's not allow feelings of unworthiness, shame, guilt, or regret to hold us back from answering God's call.

GLEANING INSIGHT FROM A BIBLE BEAUTY

Mary is a beautiful example of surrendering to God's call.

Mary must've been dreaming about what life would be like once she married Joseph. Since they were betrothed—which was more binding than being engaged is today—they were considered married in the eyes of the law, but they couldn't live together as husband and wife until after their wedding. Mary probably thought she and Joseph would live a simple life. She was just an ordinary gal marrying a carpenter.

But God had called Mary to honor Him in a very extraordinary way.

Mary must've been startled by the angel Gabriel's visitation. His first words to her were that she was highly favored by God. Then after telling Mary not to fear, he announced that she would be overshadowed by the Holy Spirit and give birth to the long-awaited Messiah.

Mary was surely in awe of this extreme call on her life.

Instead of backing down and refusing God's call, she humbly surrendered her plans and submitted to God's will.

Mary would risk losing her reputation, her fiancé, and possibly even her life, but she obeyed and trusted God anyway.

Mary's faith journey was far from easy. She most likely gave birth to Jesus in a stable, and she placed her precious newborn in a manger (a feeding container for animals). She and Joseph would flee to Egypt to find temporary refuge because King Herod wanted to kill Jesus. They wouldn't return to Israel until an angel assured them it was safe. They settled in Nazareth and raised Jesus in the ways of the Lord, not understanding when and how the prophecies about their special son would be fulfilled. And while Mary must've marveled at many of Jesus' miracles, including turning water into wine at the wedding in Cana, she also most likely felt the pain of being a widow, and she later had to endure the agony of watching Jesus crucified on the cross at Calvary for the sins of the world.

Mary still stayed true to God. She was undoubtedly beyond overjoyed to see Jesus risen from the dead. And what a blessing it must have been for her to be one of the disciples who received the Holy Spirit on Pentecost!

Almighty God *created* and loved Mary.

God *called* Mary to honor Him in a one-of-a-kind way.

God *chose* Mary to bear fruit.

God *conformed* Mary to the image of Christ.

God *clothed* Mary with purpose.

God *commissioned* Mary to shine and soar for Him.

DISCERNING GOD'S CALL

We're called to follow our Good Shepherd, as Jesus states in John 10:27: "My sheep listen to my voice; I know them, and they follow me."

So how can we begin to discern what God is calling us to do?

We need to line up any thought, idea, impression, nudge, prompting, or inkling we think we're feeling with the Bible.

If we think God is calling us to do something that contradicts the Bible, we need to stop right there. That's not of the Lord.

The main way God speaks to us and guides us is through the Bible, as we read in Psalm 119:105: "Your word is a lamp for my feet, a light on my path." But God also speaks to us during our prayer and worship times, through sermons, and perhaps through circumstances, people, and even dreams.

God has spoken to my heart in all those ways throughout my life.

And when God really wants to get my attention, I find that a certain Bible verse or phrase "happens" to appear on a church bulletin and then in a song and in a sermon, or someone "happens" to quote it to me. I say that God is speaking to me in surround sound.

It's important for us to take time to listen to God. Many times, God speaks to our hearts in a whisper, like He did with the prophet Elijah in 1 Kings 19:11-13:

> The LORD said, "Go out and stand on the mountain in the presence of the LORD, for the LORD is about to pass by."
>
> Then a great and powerful wind tore the mountains apart and shattered the rocks before the LORD, but the LORD was not in the wind. After the wind there was an earthquake, but the LORD was not in the earthquake. After the earthquake came a fire, but the LORD was not

in the fire. And after the fire came a gentle whisper. When Elijah heard it, he pulled his cloak over his face and went out and stood at the mouth of the cave.

Then a voice said to him, "What are you doing here, Elijah?"

The wind, earthquake, and fire may have gotten Elijah's attention, but the Lord spoke to Him in a gentle whisper (or "a still, small voice," in some translations).

May we take a break from our busy schedules and stop strategizing long enough to hear from God daily.

May we stop running from God's call and surrender to His perfect will.

REFLECTING ON BEING CALLED TO HONOR GOD

We can't outrun God's love or His call on our lives.

God calls us until He gets our attention.

Whether He calls us when we're little girls, young adults, or more mature women, our response is required.

And whether He calls us to do seemingly ordinary tasks or extraordinary exploits, let's remember that our first call is to love and worship God.

Is your heart feeling stirred by the passion God has placed inside you to make a difference in this world? Are you feeling God calling you to honor Him in a specific way? If so, what is that God-given dream that's stirring inside you? Why not stop and bask in that unique assignment or task you feel God calling you to?

When God created and called you, He knew what He was doing. You were created with a divine purpose. Are you ready to continue discovering and daring to live your God-given dreams?

REFLECTION QUESTIONS

I hope these questions will help stir your heart. You can use them as journal prompts or as discussion questions with your small group.

1. After reading how Samuel, Noah, Moses, Gideon, Isaiah, and Peter reacted when God called them, which Bible character can you relate to the most and why?

2. How does Mary's story inspire you and demonstrate that almighty God has called you to honor Him?

3. What godly desires and dreams has God placed in your heart?

4. What needs do you feel drawn to meet at home, at work, at church, or in your community? Why?

5. What concerns keep you up at night? Why?

6. What is one key takeaway or insight you learned from this chapter?

7. What's one faith step you can prayerfully commit to taking this week to get closer to living your God-given dreams?

ACTION STEP

Do you remember when God first called you to follow Him? How did He speak to your heart? Did He speak through a Bible verse, a family member, a dream, or some other way? How did you know it was God calling you, and how did you feel about being called? Share briefly about it in your journal.

PRAYER AND PRAISE

Lord, thank You for calling me to honor You! Please continue revealing Your call on my life, and help me to say yes. Forgive me for doubting or ignoring Your call. Today, I'm praising You and praying for . . .

CHAPTER 3

Chosen to Bear Fruit

✦   ✦

*You did not choose me, but I chose you and appointed you so that
you might go and bear fruit—fruit that will last—and so that
whatever you ask in my name the Father will give you.*

JOHN 15:16

ON A CONSTRUCTION SITE in Brazil's famed Amazon
jungle, I was helping my teammates slide in windows,
move fifty-pound placas (concrete slabs) and hundreds of
roof tiles, and fill little cracks in the walls with caulk. And
I was painting until my arms were numb.

Nonhandy me had no business being at any construction site. And squeamish city-girl me had no reason to
be out there in the wild. I'm pretty sure I saw a snake
slithering in the grass not far enough from where I was
working, but I'm not positive because I ran away before I
could verify what I had seen.

I had no reason to leave everything behind to help

build a church along a tributary of the Amazon River. But as I slept in my hammock on a boat, and as I did my small part to bring this church to life, I knew I was right in the center of God's will for my life at that moment.

How did I get here?

I didn't grow up around missionaries or hearing missionary stories.

I had always wanted to travel, but my goals involved seeing all the Olympic stadiums—not doing manual labor in the Amazon jungle.

But a humble and persistent Brazilian pastor had been praying for seven years for this church to be built in this community.

God chose me to be one of seven women on our church's ten-member team for this extreme short-term mission trip. It didn't matter that I was one of the youngest on the team or that the only building skill I had was assembling furniture.

God has a sense of humor.

Although there were plenty of reasons why I shouldn't go (including that I had to take time off work, leave everyone behind except teammates I barely knew, get a yellow fever shot, and take giant malaria pills—not to mention the anacondas, piranhas, and other perils I could encounter in the Amazon jungle), I knew God was calling me to this mission. I was drawn by knowing that during our second week we would be visiting people's homes and sharing the gospel with them.

I'm so glad I said yes to this adventure with God!

When God asked me to lay down my journalism career, I didn't have a plan B. I didn't have any delusions of grandeur.

I had to pray and walk by faith to try to figure out what to do next.

I soon became an English teacher at a Christian middle school. I found it refreshing to be in a Christian work environment, but quite challenging to work with some 125 students each day.

Teaching middle schoolers definitely stretched me out of my comfort zone. I started a school newspaper with my students, which was my way of using my writing background in that season.

My prayer life grew that year. Although I had been delaying getting baptized because I had been baptized as a child, I finally decided to take the plunge and publicly declare my decision for Christ in front of my family and friends. What a glorious day!

After teaching for a year, I became a communications specialist at a nonprofit affiliated with Columbia University. Again I was stretched beyond my journalism training. I gained so many skills in the fields of communications, marketing, and fundraising. I didn't think any of those skills could ever translate into Kingdom work.

As I explored different career options, I also grew tremendously in my faith.

By then, I was one of the leaders of a Bible-study group for young adults and had taken many Bible classes at my church.

It was during a vacation to Israel that I felt the Lord calling me to be an evangelist.

Private and introverted me? I barely spoke about God or faith to others. But I felt God had chosen me to help spread the Good News of Jesus to anyone who would listen.

There was something about traveling from New York City, the Crossroads of the World, to the crossroads of the world's three major religions that stirred my heart.

Before the tour ended, a pastor in the group prayed that God would use me as an evangelist.

I came back home to New York on fire to talk about Jesus. Since I had left journalism, my writing had been in hiding. I was content just journaling. I also enjoyed writing little care notes to our small-group members. Those notes were the only way I could imagine using my writing to help others.

It was my teacher for a spiritual-gifts class who recognized that my writing skills and my evangelism gift were a great combination.

That sounded lovely, but I had no road map for what to do next. This was before blogging and social media, so I couldn't see many outlets for my writing.

I did write for a local Christian newspaper, interviewed Christian celebrities, and even wrote a front-page story, but God reminded me that this was still journalism and asked me to lay it down too. Yikes!

For some reason, the story of Moses and his staff resonated with me (see Exodus 4:2-5). God asked Moses what was in his hand, then told him to throw down his staff—only to have him pick it up again after seeing how God would use it for His purposes. I started to feel that one day God would ask me to pick up my pen and write for His glory.

I felt drawn to write and speak about God and faith.

My trip to Israel and the spiritual gifts class I took helped confirm that God had created, called, and chosen me to be an encourager and an evangelist.

Me? The one who only wanted to write about elite athletes and work at magazines?

Over the years, I spoke to family, friends, and coworkers about Jesus, bought many of them Bibles, and invited them to church and other Christian events. Some received Jesus.

Others remained curious and asked me to pray for them in their times of need.

I also facilitated classes for new believers and baptismal candidates and helped lead evangelism classes and outreaches. I trained as a volunteer chaplain and served as a prayer counselor for a Billy Graham crusade and later a Luis Palau festival campaign in New York City.

After having traveled for work or vacation over the years, I felt the Lord calling me to give back by going on short-term mission trips.

And that's how I ended up in the Amazon jungle, venturing into murky water with local Brazilian kids. God called and chose me to go on five short-term mission trips to five countries. In Ecuador's Andes Mountains, we did home visits in the remote communities high among the clouds. In Ethiopia, we visited a leper colony, orphans who had HIV, and a foster home for girls, and we had an impromptu worship service by moonlight with young men living in a literal junkyard. In Honduras, we were escorted by security guards as two thousand missionaries flooded the country with God's love. In Lima, Peru, we visited schools and held evangelistic events in the plazas and parks.

My faith grew with each trip. Whether I was participating in the inauguration of the church God allowed us to help build along the Amazon River, riding a bus up the winding roads of the towering Andes, or playing with children and praying for adults in Ethiopia, Honduras, or Peru, I felt so honored to be the hands and feet and voice of Jesus.

I love that my age, gender, and background didn't matter when I was on the mission field. All that mattered was that each of us was there to be an expression of God's love. And we felt God's love through the wonderful people we met.

When God chooses you for Kingdom assignments, it may be difficult and challenging and stretch you out of your comfort zone. But there's no better place to be than in the center of God's will for your life.

When God chooses you, it doesn't matter what others think.

When I felt God calling me to write and speak for His glory, I was a little overwhelmed.

I'm a Latina from New York, not the Bible Belt.

I didn't have scores of mentors or role models who looked like me and from whom I could learn.

But I did have a role model in my mom, who was the first person in my immediate family to give her life to Christ. Mom became a founding member of a local Spanish church that was just starting out. She began serving in the church and had such a hunger to learn about the Bible that she attended a seminary at an established Spanish church for five years—and graduated.

My mom has a servant's heart, so over the years she did everything from being a greeter and usher to being a deaconess and the secretary for the governing board, teaching Sunday school and vacation Bible school, volunteering at the church's food pantry, going on outreaches to people experiencing homelessness, and making home visits to pray with and disciple people. She made the announcements at the start of some services and went on to teach and preach on special occasions, including at Friday night Bible classes and to the crowd of food-pantry attendees. She also helped lead a prayer group and even cohosted an online prayer time that aired on a local radio station.

I saw my mom faithfully serving at her local church, and I saw my sister delighting in serving as a Sunday school teacher at the church she and her family attend.

Still, I wasn't sure how to live out God's call to be a Christian communicator.

I turned to my mom, my senior pastor, and a few other trusted Christian friends and ministry leaders for guidance.

I'm grateful there was a diverse group of people who helped me along the way. They patiently listened to me and prayed for me.

Although my father may not have always understood my decisions, he was supportive.

But not everyone was cheering for me.

Many times, I felt overlooked, underestimated, or misunderstood.

I didn't realize women ministers aren't always welcome.

I didn't know Latina ministers are still quite rare in English-speaking churches.

After I had answered God's call to be a Christian communicator, I realized most event speakers or church leaders didn't look like me, and they didn't seem eager to invite me to their table. Although that could've been for a variety of reasons, I also didn't see much diversity represented in these gatherings, and people seemed to be fine with that.

I was already used to being the only Latina in my journalism classrooms or newsrooms and on my mission trips and at my jobs.

God wasn't surprised by my nationality, background, or gender when He chose me.

Women and men of different backgrounds have thanked me for the words of hope and encouragement I've shared. Some (female and male) have been in tears when they've heard me speak about God's amazing love for us. Many have said I shared exactly what they needed to hear.

I quickly tell them it must be the Holy Spirit working through me.

When God calls and chooses us, He prepares and

equips and anoints us. We'll talk more about that in chapter 5.

God works through His children as He pleases.

Let's rejoice over the words God spoke through the prophet Joel and again through Peter at Pentecost:

> "In the last days, God says,
>   I will pour out my Spirit on all people.
> Your sons and daughters will prophesy,
>   your young men will see visions,
>   your old men will dream dreams.
> Even on my servants, both men and women,
>   I will pour out my Spirit in those days,
>   and they will prophesy."

ACTS 2:17-18

CHOSEN BY GOD TO BEAR FRUIT

We may feel hidden, anonymous, or invisible. We may feel ignored or rejected or misunderstood by our family, peers, or society.

Can I fill you in on some great news?

The third truth in the Six Cs of Transformation is that God has chosen us to bear fruit for Him.

Almighty God sees and loves us, and guess what? God chose you and me!

God chooses us with all our flaws, faults, and fears. We are beloved, blessed, and beautiful in God's sight. Jesus chose us long before we even noticed Him. There's nothing we can say or do to change His mind about us or to make Him reject us.

Jesus says our connection to Him is as life-giving and vital as that of a branch to a vine:

> "I am the vine; you are the branches. If you remain in me and I in you, you will bear much fruit; apart from me you can do nothing. If you do not remain in me, you are like a branch that is thrown away and withers; such branches are picked up, thrown into the fire and burned. If you remain in me and my words remain in you, ask whatever you wish, and it will be done for you. This is to my Father's glory, that you bear much fruit, showing yourselves to be my disciples."
>
> JOHN 15:5-8

It's as we abide in Christ that we gain the nourishment and strength and grace we need for all that He calls us to do. Apart from Him, we can do nothing of lasting value.

Being the great gardener that He is, God takes His

time nurturing and pruning us as we start to display the fruit of the Spirit mentioned in Galatians 5:22-23: "The fruit of the Spirit is love, joy, peace, forbearance, kindness, goodness, faithfulness, gentleness and self-control. Against such things there is no law."

We'll talk more in the next chapter about how God is perfecting us. For now, let's remember that we're to bear good fruit for the Kingdom, and that includes growing in the fruit of the Spirit.

BEARING KINGDOM FRUIT

Another step to daring to live your God-given dreams is acknowledging that God has chosen you to colabor with Him.

God chose us to be His loving hands, feet, mouth, and more in this world. God has ordained us to fulfill certain Kingdom assignments. If you've ever thought you didn't have any special gifts or talents, think again.

> There are different kinds of gifts, but the same Spirit distributes them. There are different kinds of service, but the same Lord. There are different kinds of working, but in all of them and in everyone it is the same God at work.

1 CORINTHIANS 12:4-6

God may have given you the ability to sing, dance, write, lead, speak, or teach. Ask God to show you how He'd like you to use those gifts to serve Him.

It's easy to be tempted to compare with, compete with, or copy someone else's gift, but let's instead remember that God is creative and generous. He has plenty of gifts and talents for all His children.

When I first started meeting people at church, I would hear them talk about their "ministries," and it made me wonder how they were assigned their ministries. I wondered if I had missed a meeting where ministries were handed out. I gradually learned that God has given each of us different Kingdom assignments, or ministries. When we accept Jesus as Lord and Savior, He blesses us with at least one spiritual gift to carry out those assignments.

Scripture offers a window into what kinds of spiritual gifts are available to believers. For example, take 1 Corinthians 12:7-11:

> Now to each one the manifestation of the Spirit
> is given for the common good. To one there is
> given through the Spirit a message of wisdom, to
> another a message of knowledge by means of the
> same Spirit, to another faith by the same Spirit,
> to another gifts of healing by that one Spirit, to
> another miraculous powers, to another prophecy,

to another distinguishing between spirits, to
another speaking in different kinds of tongues,
and to still another the interpretation of tongues.
All these are the work of one and the same Spirit,
and he distributes them to each one, just as he
determines.

We don't earn our spiritual gifts. The Holy Spirit distributes them as He determines.

In Romans 12:3-8, the apostle Paul reminds us that all spiritual gifts are necessary. We all belong to the same body of Christ. We're to use our gifts according to our faith, and with generosity and diligence and cheerfulness:

By the grace given me I say to every one of you:
Do not think of yourself more highly than you
ought, but rather think of yourself with sober
judgment, in accordance with the faith God has
distributed to each of you. For just as each of us
has one body with many members, and these
members do not all have the same function,
so in Christ we, though many, form one body,
and each member belongs to all the others. We
have different gifts, according to the grace given
to each of us. If your gift is prophesying, then
prophesy in accordance with your faith; if it is

serving, then serve; if it is teaching, then teach;
if it is to encourage, then give encouragement;
if it is giving, then give generously; if it is to
lead, do it diligently; if it is to show mercy,
do it cheerfully.

Ephesians 4:11-13 says Jesus placed apostles, prophets, evangelists, pastors, and teachers in the church to help build up His body so we can mature in our faith, become more Christlike, and minister to others as He did.

Serving, teaching, encouraging, giving, leading, and showing mercy are just some of the gifts available to believers.

I found it so helpful and affirming to discover my spiritual gifts by taking a class and filling out spiritual-gifts surveys. These things confirmed that I was already using some of my gifts and helped me understand how God had wired me to serve Him. You may want to take a spiritual-gifts class at your church or speak with your pastor or a trusted ministry leader to learn more. There are also books about the different spiritual gifts. You might even want to take a free spiritual-gifts survey online.

Our gifts don't belong to us. Our gifts and talents are to be shared with others. We truly are blessed to be a blessing.

RESPONDING TO BEING CHOSEN BY GOD

Being chosen by God to bear fruit is an amazing honor, privilege, and responsibility. As we read in Luke 12:48, to whom much is given, much is required.

One Sunday, as I pondered how I would do all the wonderful works a prophetic pastor had spoken over me (that confirmed my calling), a sister in Christ came over to me and "happened" to quote Zechariah 4:6 to me:

> "'Not by might nor by power, but by my Spirit,'
> says the LORD Almighty."

What a great reminder that it's not about me and how much I can accomplish for God! It's about yielding to the Holy Spirit so He can empower me and work through me.

God can open doors that no human can shut, so don't give up. God's yes will make it possible for you to achieve all that He's planned for you, in His perfect way. God will provide divine connections and the right opportunities for you along the journey.

How can we prepare for all that God has ordained for us to do? We start by surrendering to God's plan. In Proverbs 16:9 we read:

> In their hearts humans plan their course,
> but the LORD establishes their steps.

We're not called to "make things happen" or "figure things out." We're called to trust God and to follow our Good Shepherd. We're called to abide in the Vine to bear good fruit.

Planning is good and necessary, but write your plans in pencil.

Let's rely on the Holy Spirit to order our steps.

Our job is to follow God wholeheartedly. God's job is to accomplish His divine will for our lives.

May Proverbs 3:5-6 be a lifeline for us:

Trust in the LORD with all your heart
    and lean not on your own understanding;
in all your ways submit to him,
    and he will make your paths straight.

When we keep God first, everything else comes into proper perspective.

GLEANING INSIGHT FROM A BIBLE BEAUTY

Deborah was a prophet, wife, judge, leader, and poet. She wore many hats, and she wore them well. As a prophet, she spoke for God to His people. As a ruler and judge, she helped keep order and decided right from wrong for the Israelites based on God's laws.

Deborah lived during the time of the judges, when

everyone did what seemed right in their own eyes. It was a time of great lawlessness and rebellion against God. It was a never-ending cycle of the Israelites rebelling, falling into idolatry, being oppressed by foreigners, and crying out to God, then God raising up a judge to deliver them . . . only for the Israelites to repeat the cycle of rebelling and worshiping foreign gods.

At the time Deborah ruled, Jabin, the king of Canaan, had oppressed the Israelites for twenty years. When God was ready to deliver His people, He chose to reveal His plans to Deborah. This wise woman didn't stay cowering under the Palm of Deborah (aptly named after her), going about her regular duties and hoping God would pick someone else for the assignment. She courageously told Barak to take his troops and go to battle against Sisera, the commander of Jabin's army. God had guaranteed them the victory against Sisera's men and their nine hundred iron chariots.

How did Barak respond to this great news?

He wouldn't go to war unless Deborah went with him.

Deborah agreed, but she declared God would deliver their enemy, Sisera, into the hands of a woman.

Barak summoned ten thousand men to fight Jabin's army. At Deborah's declaration that God was with them, Barak's men charged into battle. God gave Barak the victory over Jabin's army, and He gave the Israelites the victory over Sisera himself with the help of another fearless female named Jael.

When God chose Deborah to reveal His plan to His people, she didn't shrink back in fear. She rose to the occasion. She took God at His word and told Barak to go to battle. Everything she told Barak came true.

Deborah recorded the victory in a song so future generations would know how God had delivered His people.

Deborah's obedience to God's plan helped usher in forty years of peace for the Israelites.

Deborah is the only female judge mentioned in the book of Judges.

Although we don't know whether she had children, Deborah has gone down in history as a mother in Israel who cared for and led the Israelites with great wisdom and courage.

Almighty God *created* and loved Deborah.

God *called* Deborah to honor Him.

God *chose* Deborah to bear fruit and help deliver His people from oppression.

God *conformed* Deborah to the image of Christ.

God *clothed* Deborah with purpose.

God *commissioned* Deborah to shine and soar for Him.

STRUGGLING WITH BEING CHOSEN BY GOD

When God chose us, He knew everything about our past, present, and future. Nothing surprises Him. He knows our insecurities, quirks, hurts, wounds, struggles, sins . . . and He still chose us. We're not off the hook for fulfilling our callings.

If you're familiar with Jonah's story in the Bible, you know Jonah couldn't outrun God's assignment for him.

Let's be willing vessels to be used by God as He pleases.

Whether we feel up for the task or struggle with imposter syndrome, let's remember:

- God doesn't follow the world's ways. He has His own reasons for choosing us, as Paul pointed out in 1 Corinthians 1:26-31:

    Brothers and sisters, think of what you were when you were called. Not many of you were wise by human standards; not many were influential; not many were of noble birth. But God chose the foolish things of the world to shame the wise; God chose the weak things of the world to shame the strong. God chose the lowly things of this world and the despised things—and the things that are not—to nullify the things that are, so that no one may boast before him. It is because of him that you are in

Christ Jesus, who has become for us wisdom from God—that is, our righteousness, holiness and redemption. Therefore, as it is written: "Let the one who boasts boast in the Lord."

- Whether we feel God calling us to seemingly big or little assignments, we must remain humble, as James 4:10 encourages us to do: "Humble yourselves before the Lord, and he will lift you up." God doesn't want us getting puffed up with pride in our degrees, our training, or our experience. Those things are good and helpful for our Kingdom work, but we should keep in mind that "God opposes the proud but shows favor to the humble" (James 4:6).

- We're to do all things with gusto, even when the spotlight isn't on us or we aren't getting the recognition we think we deserve. God sees us serving and giving wholeheartedly, as Matthew 6:3-4 reminds us: "When you give to the needy, do not let your left hand know what your right hand is doing, so that your giving may be in secret. Then your Father, who sees what is done in secret, will reward you."

REFLECTING ON BEING CHOSEN BY GOD

Are things becoming clearer as you see how almighty God created you, called you, and chose you to be His beloved, blessed, and beautiful daughter? Let's stop and soak in what we've been pondering.

God loves us unconditionally and chose us to bear fruit in His name. We are God's first choice for the Kingdom assignments He has appointed and anointed us for.

When God chooses us and gives us a vision for what He would like us to do, it's important to pray about it, ponder it, and even write it down. For example, God gave Habakkuk a message to share, and the prophet wrote it down just as God directed him:

> "Write down the revelation
> and make it plain on tablets
> so that a herald may run with it.
> For the revelation awaits an appointed time;
> it speaks of the end
> and will not prove false.
> Though it linger, wait for it;
> it will certainly come
> and will not delay."
>
> HABAKKUK 2:2-3

It's also good to ask mature Christians to pray for you. Perhaps they can help you decide your next steps.

When God created, called, and chose you, He was already pleased with you! But just as a sculptor continues to shape and mold and chisel away at his masterpiece, God is continuing to mold you lovingly and carefully. Are you ready to continue discovering and daring to live your God-given dreams? God is preparing you for all the good works He has planned for you.

REFLECTION QUESTIONS

I hope these questions will help stir your heart. You can use them as journal prompts or as discussion questions with your small group.

1. How does it feel to know you're God's first choice for the assignments He has for you?

2. Do you feel like you're growing in the fruit of the Spirit? If your answer is no, why not?

3. Which spiritual gifts mentioned in this chapter resonated the most with you? Why?

4. How does Deborah's story inspire you and demonstrate that almighty God chose you to bear fruit?

5. How can you bear fruit and start living your God-given dreams right where you're planted now?

6. What is one key takeaway or insight you learned from this chapter?

7. What's one faith step you can prayerfully commit to taking this week to get closer to living your God-given dreams?

ACTION STEP

As you continue to discern the good works that God has appointed you to do, can you recall a specific moment when you helped someone and felt genuinely happy and fulfilled that you could assist them? What did you do? Describe your act of kindness in your journal, and record why it meant so much to you.

PRAYER AND PRAISE

Lord, thank You for choosing me to bear fruit! Please continue revealing Your plans and purposes for me. Forgive me when I doubt or give in to fear. Today, I'm praising You and praying for . . .

CHAPTER 4

Conformed to the Image of Christ

I urge you, brothers and sisters, in view of God's mercy, to offer your bodies as a living sacrifice, holy and pleasing to God—this is your true and proper worship. Do not conform to the pattern of this world, but be transformed by the renewing of your mind. Then you will be able to test and approve what God's will is—his good, pleasing and perfect will.

ROMANS 12:1-2

AFTER I CAME BACK FROM my amazing trip to Sydney, I started noticing some changes in myself.

I found that my interests changed, my circle of friends changed, the way I dressed and where I went for fun changed. Even the jokes I laughed at changed.

No one was dictating how I should act, and it wasn't that I had been an awful person beforehand. It was that the more I learned about Jesus, the more I wanted to be like Him.

When it finally dawned on me that Jesus lives inside me and goes everywhere I go, it made me rethink how I was living.

I wasn't trying to win God's love.

I was overwhelmed that God had forgiven my wayward ways.

It was God's amazing love for me and my love for Him that compelled me to keep growing in my Christian walk.

Once we've had an encounter with the Lord, we're never quite the same.

As I studied the Bible, read books, prayed, started going to church, surrounded myself with Christian friends, and began serving in various ways at church, I gained a new perspective.

I really was a new creation, as it says in 2 Corinthians 5:17: "Therefore, if anyone is in Christ, the new creation has come: The old has gone, the new is here!" I was now trying to live according to God's standards.

I'm grateful that my immediate familia surrendered to Jesus' leading because it led to a beautiful restoration with my dear dad. Over the years, the Lord helped heal the bitterness and anger between all of us.

During these "bonus years," we got to spend a few holidays and vacations together. That would have been unimaginable in previous years. But God allowed us all to move past our brokenness and enjoy years of joy and peace together.

It wasn't perfect, but we embraced this second chance

and were grateful for how God restored the years and the peace the enemy had tried to rob from us.

My dad was curious about the changes he saw in our familia and was open to learning more about our newfound faith. Over the years, my dear dad would gladly come to church with me. In those days, we'd have impromptu Bible studies in the park after service. He happily attended my sister's church whenever we visited her family. I even had the joy of traveling with my dad twice throughout his beloved Ecuador. Those are precious moments I will always treasure. Our trips helped me bond with my dad and embrace that side of my Latina heritage.

Just a few years before his promotion to heaven, we had the honor of witnessing my dad accept Jesus as his Lord and Savior on one glorious Christmas night.

What the enemy means for evil, God can truly turn for good. Sure, living like Jesus is often challenging, but oh, the joy and rewards we experience on the other side of obedience!

Living like Jesus includes doing a lot of soul searching and relying on the Holy Spirit to lovingly point out areas where we need to repent or change the direction we're heading.

That's not popular in today's culture, but it's so necessary for God's children to yield to Him as He molds and shapes us. It takes humility and trust in God, and it also takes courage.

That annoying person at work or the situation that's irritating you or those obstacles you're facing? They all have a purpose.

God can use anyone and everyone around us and any circumstance, good or bad, to conform us to the image of Christ.

I don't want to minimize anything you've been through. I do want to encourage you that God is right there with you, and He sees the full picture of your life.

Everything we go through may not be good, but God can turn everything around for our good. As God heals us from that struggle or heartache or challenge we've been through, we can have compassion and help comfort and strengthen others going through similar experiences.

Thankfully, we don't have to earn God's love, but we do need to follow His lead.

God left us detailed instructions in His bestselling book of all time, the Bible, and He provides sufficient grace for us to make it through each day.

BEING SET APART FOR GOD

The fourth truth in the Six Cs of Transformation is that God is conforming us to the image of Jesus.

Almighty God has created us, called us, and chosen us

to worship Him, delight in Him, and honor Him. God delights in lavishing His extravagant love on us.

We are His exquisite masterpieces. We are His precious handiwork and His lovely handmaidens. We're not meant to be like the world and to settle for its standards. We're called to live by God's standards, which we find in the Bible.

God has set us apart for His divine purposes.

God has even bigger plans for us than helping us fulfill our Kingdom assignments.

God desires us to resemble Jesus. Our Christlike character will develop over time as we surrender to God's will and work in our lives.

Salvation happens in an instant. The moment we receive Jesus as our Lord and Savior and repent and surrender our lives to Him, we receive Jesus' forgiveness of our sins and His gift of eternal life in heaven with God.

But how come we don't get ushered into heaven as soon as we accept Jesus?

Because God is preparing us for our heavenly home. And He has divine plans for us while we're still here on earth.

Sanctification, or being conformed to the image of Christ, happens every day of our lives.

Thinking and acting and reacting like Jesus doesn't happen in an instant. God isn't in a rush. God is patiently molding and shaping us. Let's trust His loving hands. His ways and thoughts are higher than ours.

We're called to consecrate (or devote) ourselves to God.

We're called to seek to know and love and worship and serve God all the days of our lives.

If we want to know God's will and unique purpose for our lives, we need to spend time with Him in prayer and to read, meditate on, and apply Scripture. We must align our thoughts with the Word of God. Our role model for living the Christian life shouldn't be found on the stage or screen. Our ultimate role model is found in the pages of the Bible—Jesus.

The Bible is God's love letter to us, so it reveals His heartbeat. We can learn what pleases God and what He warns us against. God's Word is the highest standard of truth. Let's believe what God says more than what others say.

Let's declare the promises of God aloud.

Read God's Word. Recite God's Word. Recount God's Word. Receive God's Word.

The world may want us to believe that we're not enough, that we don't have the right background or quali-fications, that we don't have the right looks or speak the right way. The world may cause us to question our worth. We may be tempted to get trapped in an endless cycle of comparison and envy and jealousy. But let's not fall for the enemy's schemes.

Let's see ourselves the way God sees us and continue to dare to live our God-given dreams!

In this chapter, we're exploring Scripture's teaching about what it looks like to live for Christ. It's a challenging chapter, but prayerfully stick with it.

MATTERS OF THE HEART

A crucial step to daring to live your God-given dreams is trusting God as He molds and shapes you into the image of Jesus. That may seem challenging and uncomfortable at times, but God is more interested in our inner lives than in any good work we could ever accomplish in His name. We can rest assured that God is conforming us to Christ's image with His utmost love for us in mind.

Developing Christlike character starts with a heart check. Proverbs 4:23 tells us, "Above all else, guard your heart, for everything you do flows from it."

It's vital that we guard our hearts. God wants us to love Him and others and to serve others with right motives. When we carry around hurt, offense, bitterness, or resentment, all these things get stored inside us and are on display through our actions and words. In some cases, they're evident in our *lack* of actions or words.

We may not even notice that we're carrying all this

baggage, but God knows, and He's chiseling away at us to heal and restore those areas of brokenness just as a sculptor chisels away any imperfections in his precious sculptures.

God wants our hearts to reflect His heart.

King David was far from perfect, but both the Old and New Testaments refer to him as a man after God's heart.

God didn't commend King David for his intellect, courage, or strength, which are all important qualities, but for his obedient heart. That speaks volumes.

God wants us to want Him with our whole hearts, and He wants us to have willing hearts that say yes to Him. King David knew the importance of allowing God to search his heart. We can make Psalm 139:23-24 our prayer as well: "Search me, God, and know my heart; test me and know my anxious thoughts. See if there is any offensive way in me, and lead me in the way everlasting."

There are countless Bible verses that speak about the heart.

Someone once prayed Matthew 5:8 over me, and I cherish it: "Blessed are the pure in heart, for they will see God."

In 2 Chronicles 16:9 we read that God searches and strengthens the human heart: "The eyes of the LORD range throughout the earth to strengthen those whose hearts are fully committed to him."

According to this verse, God isn't looking for the strong and mighty or for that gal who seems to have a perfect life. God is aiming to strengthen those whose hearts are fully committed to Him.

That's us!

An obedient heart is of the utmost importance to God. As 1 Samuel 15:22 tells us, obedience is better than sacrifice. We can serve and give and have perfect church attendance, but if our hearts aren't in it—or if we're doing good deeds with the wrong motives—we might be able to hide the truth from others, but not from God.

God doesn't want us to go through the motions or try to impress people or act out of duty. God wants us to delight in worshiping Him and in serving and giving.

What did King David do when God exposed his sin? He humbled himself and turned to God. His prayer recorded in Psalm 51:10 says, "Create in me a pure heart, O God, and renew a steadfast spirit within me."

Let's ask God often to search and cleanse our hearts.

BEING CONFORMED TO CHRIST'S IMAGE

Living for Christ doesn't mean we're doomed to a boring life.

On the contrary, there's nothing more satisfying than living at the center of God's will for our lives.

Being set apart for God means we rely on God to adjust any attitudes, habits, or characteristics that don't reflect our identity as God's beloved daughters.

I've got bad news and good news, so get ready. The bad news is that we're going to look at different types of sin and talk about God's discipline. The good news is that we're going to look at sin through the lens of the hope and redemption we have in Jesus.

Please don't skip through this important section.

Our character and integrity (who we are behind closed doors, or how we act when we think no one is watching) matter more to God than our good works.

We All Have Fallen Short

People don't like to talk about sin, but we can't ignore it. As the Bible says in Romans 3:22-24, we all sin:

> There is no difference between Jew and Gentile,
> for all have sinned and fall short of the glory
> of God, and all are justified freely by his grace
> through the redemption that came by Christ
> Jesus.

No one is perfect. Struggling with sin is part of the human experience. We are tempted to sin daily. Remember: Jesus was tempted in every way but was without sin. He understands our weaknesses and can deliver us from our sinful ways when we ask Him for help.

Ephesians 4:29-32 gives us a glimpse of how Christians should live:

> Do not let any unwholesome talk come out of your mouths, but only what is helpful for building others up according to their needs, that it may benefit those who listen. And do not grieve the Holy Spirit of God, with whom you were sealed for the day of redemption. Get rid of all bitterness, rage and anger, brawling and slander, along with every form of malice. Be kind and compassionate to one another, forgiving each other, just as in Christ God forgave you.

If we're struggling with anything mentioned in this Scripture or in other Bible verses we encounter, let's not gloss over it. Instead, let's pay attention as the Holy Spirit convicts us or tells us where we're falling short.

On the other hand, let's not allow the enemy to condemn us and bury us in shame and regret. The Bible gives us good news. We have a Savior who will forgive us when we confess, repent, and ask for His forgiveness, as we read in 1 John 1:8-10:

If we claim to be without sin, we deceive ourselves
and the truth is not in us. If we confess our sins,
he is faithful and just and will forgive us our sins
and purify us from all unrighteousness. If we claim
we have not sinned, we make him out to be a liar
and his word is not in us.

When we receive God's forgiveness, He wipes our
slates clean.

Whenever old or new temptations pop up, we can run
to Jesus for help.

Jesus is our advocate, as the beloved disciple John
pointed out in 1 John 2:1-2: "My dear children, I write
this to you so that you will not sin. But if anybody does
sin, we have an advocate with the Father—Jesus Christ,
the Righteous One. He is the atoning sacrifice for our
sins, and not only for ours but also for the sins of the
whole world."

God knows we're human and prone to wander and
be tempted by sin. He hasn't left us alone or defenseless.
Jesus, who is perfect and sinless, paid the penalty for our
sins. Let's grab hold of that truth.

We were still sinners when Christ died for us. We don't
deserve that kind of mercy or grace. There's no way we can
repay that debt, and Jesus doesn't expect us to. We can't do
enough good works to earn God's forgiveness. We need to

receive God's gift of forgiveness and live like Him by the power of the Holy Spirit.

Talking about sin isn't easy, but the sooner we confess our sin to Jesus, the sooner we'll experience His forgiveness. Romans 8:1-2 states: "There is now no condemnation for those who are in Christ Jesus, because through Christ Jesus the law of the Spirit who gives life has set you free from the law of sin and death."

Growing and Maturing in Christ

Ever wonder why the Bible doesn't gloss over people's sin? For example, we read about how the Israelites rebelled against God and committed idolatry and sexual immorality and so much more. Their sins were recorded to serve as warnings to us, so that we could see ourselves in God's bigger story, understand our need for Jesus' sacrifice, and long for the grace He provides.

There were consequences for the Israelites' sinful ways, and there are consequences for our sinful ways.

But we don't have to follow in their rebellious footsteps.

Let's learn from the Israelites' example. Instead of grumbling and complaining against God and trying to test Him, let's trust and obey Him even during the hard times. As we face different trials and temptations, we will grow and mature, and our Christlike character will continue to develop.

Let's look at some of the many benefits of this process. According to Scripture, it's a sign of love when God disciplines us:

In your struggle against sin, you have not yet resisted to the point of shedding your blood. And have you completely forgotten this word of encouragement that addresses you as a father addresses his son? It says,

"My son, do not make light of the Lord's discipline,
   and do not lose heart when he rebukes you,
because the Lord disciplines the one he loves,
   and he chastens everyone he accepts as his son."

Endure hardship as discipline; God is treating you as his children. For what children are not disciplined by their father? If you are not disciplined—and everyone undergoes discipline—then you are not legitimate, not true sons and daughters at all. Moreover, we have all had human fathers who disciplined us and we respected them

for it. How much more should we submit to the
Father of spirits and live! They disciplined us
for a little while as they thought best; but God
disciplines us for our good, in order that we may
share in his holiness. No discipline seems pleasant
at the time, but painful. Later on, however, it
produces a harvest of righteousness and peace for
those who have been trained by it.

HEBREWS 12:4-11

God disciplines us, or teaches and trains us, because
we are His children. We don't have to fear God. He disciplines us with love so that we can become more like Him.

Like Father, like daughter.

If thinking of God as your heavenly Father is difficult because of your experience with your earthly parents,
remember that God loves you unconditionally. God is
love, and "[His] perfect love drives out fear" (1 John 4:18).
Empowered by God's love, we can live out the divine call
on our lives.

May Romans 12:1-2 be a guiding passage for us all as
we try to discover God's will for our lives:

I urge you, brothers and sisters, in view of God's
mercy, to offer your bodies as a living sacrifice,
holy and pleasing to God—this is your true

and proper worship. Do not conform to the pattern of this world, but be transformed by the renewing of your mind. Then you will be able to test and approve what God's will is—his good, pleasing and perfect will.

May we worship God with our whole being and be a living sacrifice unto Him. And may we surrender to God as He renews our minds so our thinking aligns with His.

Scripture tells us that we're called to love God, to love our neighbors as ourselves, to serve and pray for one another, to help the poor and needy and oppressed, and to encourage one another. We're called to keep the Ten Commandments and the teachings of Jesus, including His instruction to love our enemies and pray for those who persecute us. We're called to pray for our leaders. We're called to act justly, kindly, and mercifully toward others, including widows, orphans, foreigners, the elderly, the sick, the imprisoned—the least of these. We're called to extend grace to others, offer hospitality, give generously, and forgive one another.

Much of this can seem impossible or contrary to our human nature, but God's grace is sufficient. God will help us walk in His ways.

Remember: When we sin or miss the mark in some area, we shouldn't hide from what we've done. Instead, let's ask the Holy Spirit to lovingly convict us of our sinful ways so we can repent, ask Jesus for forgiveness, and start fresh.

GLEANING INSIGHT FROM A BIBLE BEAUTY

Mary of Magdala (also known as Mary Magdalene) was tormented by seven demons. Her life was likely filled with fear, pain, chaos, and trauma until she met Jesus. What unspeakable joy and relief and healing she must have felt when Jesus delivered her once and for all! She was so grateful and indebted to Jesus that she dedicated her life to serving, supporting, and worshiping her Messiah. Mary Magdalene was among the women who traveled from town to town with the twelve disciples as Jesus preached the Good News of the Kingdom of God.

Mary had a front-row seat to Jesus' ministry, and it left an indelible mark on her. The more time she spent with Jesus while He was here on earth, the more she was conformed to His image and character.

Mary, standing by Jesus' mother and other grieving women, witnessed the torture Jesus endured on the cross.

Jesus' disciples may have scattered, but Mary was one of the few who stayed. Not even death could separate her from her beloved Lord and teacher.

Mary was there when Jesus was placed in the tomb.

Mary's undying devotion to her Lord compelled her to

head to Jesus' tomb early that first Easter morning. God honored her faithfulness.

Mary Magdalene got to see the risen Jesus that first Resurrection morning.

Jesus charged her with telling the other disciples the ultimate Good News. She was one of the first to proclaim that Jesus is alive!

Mary, who was once possessed by demons, was transformed into a woman consumed with love for Jesus.

Almighty God *created* and loved Mary Magdalene.

God *called* Mary Magdalene to honor Him.

God *chose* Mary Magdalene to bear fruit.

God *conformed* Mary Magdalene to the image of Christ.

God *clothed* Mary Magdalene with purpose.

God *commissioned* Mary Magdalene to share the Good News and shine and soar for Him.

CHALLENGES TO BEING CONFORMED TO THE IMAGE OF CHRIST

Living for Christ and following God's will can be challenging, but it's not impossible. The process of being transformed into the image of Jesus may seem grueling or feel like punishment sometimes, but God's grace is always available to help us.

Scripture shows us how Jesus, our perfect role model, lived while here on earth. When the religious leaders began to persecute Him, Jesus said to them, "Very truly I tell you, the Son can do nothing by himself; he can do only what he sees his Father doing, because whatever the Father does the Son also does" (John 5:19).

Jesus lived to please His Father and to follow His divine assignment. Like Father, like Son. We can learn from Jesus' stellar example.

When He was tempted by the enemy in the wilderness, He fought back by quoting Scripture. We, too, can stand on God's Word when we face temptations.

When Jesus struggled in the garden of Gethsemane, He ultimately surrendered to God's will, saying, "Father, if you are willing, take this cup from me; yet not my will, but yours be done" (Luke 22:42).

Jesus displayed His supreme love for His Father and for us by following God's plan and laying down His life for us.

May we make it our desire to live God's will, not ours.

It takes patience, perseverance, and prayer to live according to God's will. We're called to pray for God's will to be accomplished, as in the Lord's Prayer: "Your kingdom come, your will be done, on earth as it is in heaven" (Matthew 6:10).

The apostle Paul knew he was called and chosen to point people to Christ. He knew it was better to live for Christ than to follow his own agenda.

Paul's words in Galatians 2:20 can reflect our lifestyle as well: "I have been crucified with Christ and I no longer live, but Christ lives in me. The life I now live in the body, I live by faith in the Son of God, who loved me and gave himself for me."

Living for God includes living according to His standards. God doesn't change. God's standards still stand. His Word endures forever.

Sin may seem fun for a season, but it usually ends in the death and destruction of dreams, health, relationships, and more.

As James, Jesus' half brother, bluntly puts it in James 4:7-8: "Submit yourselves, then, to God. Resist the devil, and he will flee from you. Come near to God and he will come near to you. Wash your hands, you sinners, and purify your hearts, you double-minded."

Thank God we have the Holy Spirit to help us live for Christ.

REFLECTING ON BEING CONFORMED TO CHRIST'S IMAGE

Way to go for making it through this chapter! Are you getting a better understanding of why our inner thoughts and character matter so much to God? We are God's beloved, blessed, and beautiful daughters. Almighty God created us with extravagant love, called us to honor Him, chose us to bear fruit, and is taking great care to conform us to Jesus' image.

Let's reflect on what we've been talking about in this chapter.

Being God's children is a high calling, as 1 Peter 1:14-21 tells us:

> As obedient children, do not conform to the evil desires you had when you lived in ignorance. But just as he who called you is holy, so be holy in all you do; for it is written: "Be holy, because I am holy."
>
> Since you call on a Father who judges each person's work impartially, live out your time as foreigners here in reverent fear. For you know that it was not with perishable things such as silver or gold that you were redeemed from the empty way of life handed down to you from your ancestors, but with the precious blood of Christ, a lamb without blemish or defect. He was chosen before the creation of the world, but was revealed in these last times for your sake. Through him you believe in God, who raised him from the dead and glorified him, and so your faith and hope are in God.

We're called to be holy, or set apart, just as God our Father is holy.

We were bought with a great price, the precious blood of Jesus.

Our lives are not our own.

We are the temple of God.

Our pasts don't define us.

Our present negative circumstances don't determine our future.

We are brand-new in the eyes of the Lord.

Let's make Psalm 19:14 our hearts' cry:

May these words of my mouth and this meditation
of my heart
be pleasing in your sight,
LORD, my Rock and my Redeemer.

Let's hide God's Word in our hearts so we won't sin against Him.

God has equipped you for His divine purpose. God has empowered you as you dare to live your God-given dreams!

REFLECTION QUESTIONS

I hope these questions will help stir your heart. You can use them as journal prompts or as discussion questions with your small group.

1. Do you struggle with receiving Jesus' forgiveness for your past sins? If so, why?

2. Are there sins you need Jesus to set you free from right now?

3. What's one sin that God has already set you free from? How has that affected who you are today, and how has it influenced which population or cause you feel called to serve?

4. How does Mary Magdalene's story inspire you and demonstrate that almighty God conforms us to the image of Christ?

5. What Bible verse helps you fight any temptations you may be facing?

6. What is one key takeaway or insight you learned from this chapter?

7. What's one faith step you can prayerfully commit to taking this week to get closer to living your God-given dreams?

ACTION STEP

Read 1 Corinthians 6:18-20; Galatians 5:13-21; and Colossians 3:5-11. Ask God to search your heart, and write a prayer in response.

PRAYER AND PRAISE

Lord, thank You for continuing to conform me to the image of Jesus! Forgive me when I stumble and sin. Help me receive Your grace and mercy so I can be holy as You are holy. Today, I'm praising You and praying for . . .

CHAPTER 5

Clothed with Purpose

Put on the full armor of God, so that when the day of evil comes, you may be able to stand your ground, and after you have done everything, to stand. Stand firm then, with the belt of truth buckled around your waist, with the breastplate of righteousness in place, and with your feet fitted with the readiness that comes from the gospel of peace. In addition to all this, take up the shield of faith, with which you can extinguish all the flaming arrows of the evil one. Take the helmet of salvation and the sword of the Spirit, which is the word of God.

EPHESIANS 6:13-17

WHEN I LOOK BACK ON MY LIFE and my ministry experience, I see how God trained me in some of the finest schools and newsrooms as a journalist, only to pluck me out from that environment to train me during seasons of obscurity in classrooms and offices and in some of the most remote parts of the world on His mission field.

God had a purpose all along, even if I didn't always see it.

Once I started sharing some of my thoughts and reflections in emails to close friends, I was touched to see how my writing was touching them.

It was as if God had redeemed my writing.

God was calling me to write, but not about celebrities or current events.

I was to encourage people in their faith and invite them to taste and see that God really is good and faithful. I was to remind people that God loves them, that Jesus is our living hope, and that we can believe God will do the impossible.

Around that time, my church sent me and two other leaders to a series of training symposiums through The Navigators.

For me, attending the trainings meant using vacation days from work. It also meant being one of the only women as well as the only Latina in the room. During one of the breaks, I mentioned to a friend that I felt God was calling me to do something that didn't exist.

"Then create it," my friend said.

That stuck with me.

When I felt God calling me into full-time ministry, my pastor suggested I go to Bible school.

I didn't want to go. I thought I was done with school. But I went anyway. It was an important step in that season.

"God's going to write your story, and you're going to tell it," my pastor told me.

God wastes nothing. All those years of life experience and travel and training were leading somewhere.

During this season, a Christian counselor I briefly saw said she was inspired by my faith to believe God for the impossible and was encouraged by the upward trajectory of my life.

When God calls us, He also equips us.

During a prayer time with my teammates on a short-term mission trip, our leader, who was a pastor, prayed for me. He said he pictured me wearing a suit, and he told me God had given me everything I needed. He saw me as a soldier who goes ahead of the army to clear trees and make a path so the rest of the troops can advance.

I took the pastor's words to mean that God had given me His armor and had equipped me for my Kingdom assignments.

On another short-term mission trip, one of my younger team leaders was in tears as she told me she admired that God had given me a crown and that I just lay it at His feet.

We are Christ's spiritual warriors, members of His royal family, and His bride.

As we get dressed every morning, let's remember our spiritual attire.

CLOTHED IN CHRIST

The fifth truth in the Six Cs of Transformation is that God has clothed us with purpose.

As we dare to live our God-given dreams and purpose, we need to stay covered by Christ's love and power and grace and strength.

When God sees us, He sees Jesus.

According to Galatians 3:26-28, as we learned in chapter 1, we're clothed with Christ, and there's no distinction between Jew and Gentile, male and female, slave and free. This means that God doesn't discriminate against us because of our nationality, race, gender, or social status.

Colossians 3:3 states that we're hidden in Christ.

We don't need to be limited by labels or stereotypes society tries to place on us. Nor are we defined solely by nationality or political affiliation or any other trappings of this world.

Let's also not get stuck in our pasts and defined by our rocky beginnings or past sins. Jesus can redeem and redefine us.

What a powerful truth we find in Isaiah 61:10:

I delight greatly in the LORD;
    my soul rejoices in my God.
For he has clothed me with garments of salvation
    and arrayed me in a robe of his righteousness,
as a bridegroom adorns his head like a priest,
    and as a bride adorns herself with her jewels.

God has clothed us with garments of salvation, arrayed us in a robe of righteousness, and adorned us as a bride. That's better than any dress found on the red carpet. Our divine garments can't be earned; they are gifts from almighty God.

It's incredible and indescribable to know that God blesses and adorns us. If you grew up thinking that God was mad at you or waiting to punish you, take time to meditate on these precious verses:

The Spirit of the Sovereign Lord is on me,
    because the Lord has anointed me
    to proclaim good news to the poor.
He has sent me to bind up the brokenhearted,
    to proclaim freedom for the captives
    and release from darkness for the prisoners,
to proclaim the year of the Lord's favor
    and the day of vengeance of our God,
to comfort all who mourn,
    and provide for those who grieve in Zion—
to bestow on them a crown of beauty
    instead of ashes,
the oil of joy
    instead of mourning,
and a garment of praise
    instead of a spirit of despair.

They will be called oaks of righteousness,
a planting of the LORD
for the display of his splendor.

ISAIAH 61:1-3

If you feel your life has gone up in smoke, God has a crown of beauty for you.

If you've been battling grief and lamenting, God has the oil of joy for you.

If you've been struggling with despair, God has a garment of praise for you.

Let's walk in our divine wardrobe as we live out our divine purpose.

If you're walking through a dark night of the soul and battling despair or depression, I don't want to trivialize what you're going through. I encourage you to find an experienced Christian counselor or trusted pastor nearby who can help you.

We can take comfort knowing that God is near to the brokenhearted and that our weeping isn't meant to last forever, for joy comes in the morning (Psalm 30:5). God clothes us with joy, as we read later in the same psalm:

You turned my wailing into dancing;
you removed my sackcloth and clothed me
with joy,

that my heart may sing your praises and not be silent.
Lord my God, I will praise you forever.

PSALM 30:11-12

CLOTHED FOR BATTLE AND VICTORY

Once we know how much we're loved by God and adorned by His amazing grace, we can face whatever trials or obstacles appear as we dare to live our God-given dreams.

We're God's beloved, blessed, and beautiful daughters, and the enemy hates that. He hates God and is bent on harming us and stealing and destroying our futures.

Let's remember we're in a spiritual battle, as the apostle Paul points out in Ephesians 6:12:

> Our struggle is not against flesh and blood, but against the rulers, against the authorities, against the powers of this dark world and against the spiritual forces of evil in the heavenly realms.

Our supervisors, neighbors, family members, or coworkers are not our enemies. The enemy is our enemy, and he roars like a lion, looking for someone to destroy.

We shouldn't ignore the enemy and pretend he doesn't exist, but we also shouldn't fixate on him.

The enemy is no match for Jesus!

God wants us to accomplish our Kingdom purposes even more than we do.

He's the One who placed those callings on our lives and chose us for those tasks.

God has clothed us for victory.

I'm reminded of young David, who wanted to take on Goliath but couldn't fight his opponent wearing King Saul's armor:

> Then Saul dressed David in his own tunic. He put a coat of armor on him and a bronze helmet on his head. David fastened on his sword over the tunic and tried walking around, because he was not used to them.
>
> "I cannot go in these," he said to Saul, "because I am not used to them." So he took them off. Then he took his staff in his hand, chose five smooth stones from the stream, put them in the pouch of his shepherd's bag and, with his sling in his hand, approached the Philistine.
>
> 1 SAMUEL 17:38-40

Imagine how much courage it took not only to fight the towering Goliath but also to say no to wearing the king's armor. David knew that God was on his side, and he trusted his training.

God had trained the young shepherd as he guarded his father's flock in the fields. David recalled how God had rescued him from the paw of the lion and of the bear.

He was skilled in fighting with his sling, not fighting in heavy armor.

It's important for us to use the gifts and skills God has given us and not try to be someone else.

God has given us His armor. Let's wear it and use it well.

We read in Ephesians 6:14-18 about the armor God has provided for our spiritual battles:

Stand firm then, with the belt of truth buckled around your waist, with the breastplate of righteousness in place, and with your feet fitted with the readiness that comes from the gospel of peace. In addition to all this, take up the shield of faith, with which you can extinguish all the flaming arrows of the evil one. Take the helmet of salvation and the sword of the Spirit, which is the word of God.

And pray in the Spirit on all occasions with all kinds of prayers and requests. With this in mind, be alert and always keep on praying for all the Lord's people.

God has covered us from the tops of our heads to the tips of our toes. God has armed us with

- the belt of truth, so we won't fall for the enemy's lies;
- the breastplate of righteousness, so we remember our position of authority in Christ;
- feet fitted with the gospel of peace, so we can stand firm;
- the shield of faith, to guard us from the flaming arrows of the evil one;
- the helmet of salvation, representing the blood of Christ, which covers and protects us; and
- the sword of the Spirit, which is God's Word found in Scripture. This is the only weapon we need. Just as Jesus wielded Scripture against the enemy, we can declare the Word of God to our adversary. God's Word is more powerful than any double-edged sword.

Remember, the Bible doesn't say that weapons won't *be formed* against us, but that those weapons won't *succeed* in destroying us.

Please note that we don't use physical weapons for spiritual warfare. Prayer, worship, and declaring and believing God's Word are all parts of our spiritual warfare and are more powerful than we can imagine.

We're to overcome evil with good.

Thankfully, our battles are ultimately the Lord's.

Oh, that we could see the horses and chariots of fire all around us, as the prophet Elisha and his servant did, and remember that the armies of heaven are on our side!

Jesus has given us His Spirit and His armor, which empower us to remain steadfast no matter what trials we face.

We don't have to hide or cower in fear.

We can stand strong.

When the enemy throws his fiery darts and hurls accusations that God doesn't love us or that we're never going to make it, and when people try to cause us to doubt or fear or quit, we can raise our shield of faith and take courage in knowing that God is our ultimate shield and refuge.

CLOTHED AS ROYALTY

We're not just soldiers. We're also royalty because our Father sits on His throne in heaven and is the King of kings and Lord of lords. The Bible also refers to us as a royal priesthood because we serve and are set apart for the King.

I've been fascinated with crowns since childhood. Whether they were cardboard crowns from a burger joint or birthday crowns and floral wreaths for special occasions,

I loved me some crowns as a niña. I'm still somewhat fascinated with crowns, castles, and the pageantry that goes with royalty, but now I look at these things through the lens of being a beloved daughter of the King whose Kingdom has no end.

Crowns appear several times throughout Scripture to represent the rewards we'll receive in heaven for the good works we did for Christ while here on earth.

These crowns can't be bought, and they're not for us to strut around in. We're to lay them at the feet of Jesus in worship.

While we're here on earth, let's act in a way worthy of our royal calling and identity. We're seated in heavenly places with Jesus, who is seated at the right hand of God the Father. We are called to rule and reign through Him and not for our own gain and glory.

Let's use our God-given authority to represent King Jesus well and to invite others into His Kingdom.

The Bible says we are coheirs with Christ. When we remember that everything belongs to Jesus, we can trust Him to take care of all our needs.

When we remember who we are according to our spiritual DNA, we can rejoice knowing that we are royalty and that our true happily ever after awaits in heaven.

GLEANING INSIGHT FROM A BIBLE BEAUTY

Esther, also known as Hadassah, was an ordinary young lady living in the city of Susa. Esther, an orphan, had been cared for by her cousin Mordecai. They were among the Jews living in Persia (formerly Babylon) after the exile of thousands of Jews from the kingdom of Judah.

Esther likely had simple plans for her life. Her plans were interrupted when she was recruited to compete for the chance to marry King Xerxes and become the next queen. Esther, described as beautiful and lovely, is one of the few Bible characters whose physical appearance Scripture mentions, but her good looks could get her only so far. As we read, we find there's more to Esther than meets the eye.

This young woman must've felt unqualified and out of her league. She didn't come from a noble family. How could a common gal like her ever gain the king's favor? But God had chosen Esther and had clothed her with His purpose.

Esther went through the required year of beauty treatments. Per Mordecai's directive, she kept her Jewish heritage a secret. Perhaps she also learned more about Persian culture and customs and how to act like royalty.

When her time came to meet King Xerxes, Esther found favor in his sight and was crowned queen.

She didn't live happily ever after, though.

Esther soon learned that the king's top official, Haman, had convinced the king that a certain group of people throughout his empire should be annihilated. The deadly decree Haman issued on the king's behalf turned out to target none other than Esther's people, the Jews.

Esther could've kept her identity a secret and tried to save her own life, but Mordecai implored her to speak up for her people, saying that perhaps God had placed her in the palace for this exact moment.

Upon Esther's request, Mordecai asked the Jews in Susa to spend three days and nights fasting for her. On the third day of fasting with her attendants, Esther put on her royal robes and answered God's call on her life.

Esther went before the king in his inner court without being summoned, which was against the law and punishable by death. But God's favor was upon Esther as she risked her life for His people. The king granted her entrance and was ready to listen to her request.

Esther invited Xerxes and Haman to two feasts before revealing her identity as a Jew and pleading for her life and the lives of her people. She also named Haman as the mastermind behind the deadly plot. The king was furious at Haman and had him executed. He allowed Esther and Mordecai to write a new decree permitting the Jews to defend themselves on the day appointed for their annihilation. Jews still celebrate Purim in honor of how God rescued them from destruction, thanks in large part to Queen Esther taking a stand and pleading their case before the king.

Esther, who came from humble beginnings and was crowned a queen, used her royal status to help save her people. She is one of only two women to have a book of the Bible named after her.

Almighty God *created* and loved Esther.

God *called* Esther to honor Him.

God *chose* Esther to bear fruit.

God *conformed* Esther to the image of Christ.

God *clothed* Esther with royal robes and purpose.

God *commissioned* Esther to shine and soar for Him.

ADORNED FROM THE INSIDE OUT

Society may be obsessed with outward beauty—and there's nothing wrong with looking our best—but inner beauty is even more important because it's everlasting. Let's go to God's beauty school to learn what true beauty looks like.

In Psalm 34:5 we read: "Those who look to him are radiant; their faces are never covered with shame."

God's beloved daughters are radiant. We glow from the inside out, so we can skip the expensive makeup or social-media filters if we want.

Although artists throughout history have depicted Jesus in various ways, no one knows what He looked like.

It's as though Jesus didn't want us fixated on His appearance.

The prophet Isaiah shared a poignant description of Jesus hundreds of years before Christ walked the earth. He depicted Jesus, the darling of heaven and the Lamb of God, as a Suffering Servant:

> He grew up before him like a tender shoot,
>> and like a root out of dry ground.
> He had no beauty or majesty to attract us to him,
>> nothing in his appearance that we should
>>> desire him.
> He was despised and rejected by mankind,
>> a man of suffering, and familiar with pain.
> Like one from whom people hide their faces
>> he was despised, and we held him in low esteem.

ISAIAH 53:2-3

How does this description of Jesus challenge your notion of beauty?

Our culture is obsessed with skin tone and hair texture and the shape of the eyes or a person's body or height or age.

Do you think Jesus is obsessed with these things?

God doesn't have favorites. He's the One who created us in all our varying shapes and hues and hair types.

Divine beauty starts on the inside, as we read in
1 Peter 3:3-4:

> Your beauty should not come from outward
> adornment, such as elaborate hairstyles and the
> wearing of gold jewelry or fine clothes. Rather,
> it should be that of your inner self, the unfading
> beauty of a gentle and quiet spirit, which is of
> great worth in God's sight.

If we look at that passage in context, we see that Peter
was directing his comments to those who may have been
showing off their status and wealth by dressing in ways
that were considered extravagant at that time, which is
important to remember. But his point is still relevant
today: Beauty comes from the inside. Inner beauty doesn't
fade with time or go out of style.

True beauty is timeless.

As we care for our bodies and eat well and exercise
and rest and try to manage stress, let's remember that our
bodies aren't meant to last forever.

Our spirits are eternal. And our bodies will someday
be renewed.

God wants His beloved daughters to adorn themselves
with good works done out of our love for Him, as we read
in Colossians 3:12-14:

Therefore, as God's chosen people, holy and dearly loved, clothe yourselves with compassion, kindness, humility, gentleness and patience. Bear with each other and forgive one another if any of you has a grievance against someone. Forgive as the Lord forgave you. And over all these virtues put on love, which binds them all together in perfect unity.

Notice that the apostle Paul mentions wearing love so we can live out these virtues.

When we clothe ourselves with Christlike love, we can be compassionate, kind, humble, gentle, and patient.

REFLECTING ON BEING CLOTHED WITH PURPOSE

Has this chapter challenged your standards of beauty? Are you walking taller as you dare to live your God-given dreams, knowing God has clothed you with great purpose? We tend to fret and fuss about external things, but let's consider Jesus' words recorded in Matthew 6:25-34:

"Therefore I tell you, do not worry about your life, what you will eat or drink; or about your body, what you will wear. Is not life more than food, and the body more than clothes? Look at the birds of the air; they do not sow or reap or store away in barns, and yet your heavenly Father feeds them. Are you not much more valuable than they? Can any one of you by worrying add a single hour to your life?

"And why do you worry about clothes? See how the flowers of the field grow. They do not labor or spin. Yet I tell you that not even Solomon in all his splendor was dressed like one of these. If that is how God clothes the grass of the field, which is here today and tomorrow is thrown into the fire, will he not much more clothe you—you of little faith? So do not worry, saying, 'What shall we eat?' or 'What shall we drink?' or 'What shall we wear?' For the pagans run after all these things, and your heavenly Father knows that you need them. But seek first his kingdom and his righteousness, and all these things will be given to you as well. Therefore do not worry about tomorrow, for tomorrow will worry about itself. Each day has enough trouble of its own."

God doesn't want us consumed with the cares of this world. God will take care of all our needs and clothe and feed and provide for us.

Trusting God is the most beautiful thing we can do. We don't even have to fear aging. God's beloved, beautiful, and blessed daughters will live forever, and God promises to be with us from the beginning until we see Him in heaven, as we read in Isaiah 46:4: "Even to your old age and gray hairs I am he, I am he who will sustain you. I have made you and I will carry you; I will sustain you and I will rescue you."

Society may want us to spend our money trying to find the mythical fountain of youth, but we don't have to chase that fantasy.

We're to be comfortable in our skin without being vain, defined by our looks, or obsessed with how we measure up to the world's photoshopped standards of beauty. We're fearfully and wonderfully made in God's image. And God doesn't discard us because of our age.

Consider Sarah, Elizabeth, Anna, and Naomi, elderly women God loved and used in mighty ways. We can age gracefully as we make our journey to heaven, as Paul reminds us in 2 Corinthians 4:16-18:

> Therefore we do not lose heart. Though outwardly we are wasting away, yet inwardly we are being renewed day by day. For our light and momentary troubles are achieving for us an eternal glory that far outweighs them all. So we

fix our eyes not on what is seen, but on what is unseen, since what is seen is temporary, but what is unseen is eternal.

Let's rejoice that we're being inwardly renewed day by day!

Want to know the ultimate beauty secret? Spend more time gazing at Jesus, as 2 Corinthians 3:18 says: "We all, who with unveiled faces contemplate the Lord's glory, are being transformed into his image with ever-increasing glory, which comes from the Lord, who is the Spirit."

When we feel tempted to measure ourselves by the latest beauty trend, we should remember who we are in Christ. We're simply jars of clay created by the Master Potter. The true treasure is Jesus living inside us.

Let your inner beauty shine through, and remember to reflect Christ's character and behavior as you go about your days. And don't forget that the Proverbs 31 woman isn't praised for her looks or style but for her fear of the Lord. In Proverbs 31:30 we read: "Charm is deceptive, and beauty is fleeting; but a woman who fears the LORD is to be praised."

Are you feeling ready to say yes to your God-given dreams? We're coming to the final chapter in this journey of discovering and living our divine purpose.

REFLECTION QUESTIONS

I hope these questions will help stir your heart. You can use them as journal prompts or as discussion questions with your small group.

1. How does it feel to know you're clothed in God's armor?

2. How does it feel to be adorned as Christ's bride?

3. Do you struggle with striving to measure up to the world's standards of beauty? If so, why?

4. How does Esther's story inspire you and demonstrate that almighty God has clothed you with purpose?

5. What do you think God's unique purpose is for you?

6. What is one key takeaway or insight you learned from this chapter?

7. What's one faith step you can prayerfully commit to taking this week to get closer to living your God-given dreams?

ACTION STEP

Are you clothed with the following traits? Without condemnation, rate yourself from 1 to 5 (5 being the highest) in the following virtues mentioned in Colossians 3:12-14, then write a prayer in response.

Compassion	1	2	3	4	5
Kindness	1	2	3	4	5
Humility	1	2	3	4	5
Gentleness	1	2	3	4	5
Patience	1	2	3	4	5
Love	1	2	3	4	5

PRAYER AND PRAISE

Lord, thank You for clothing me with Your love, strength, and purpose! Forgive me when I rebel and walk in ways contrary to Yours. Today, I'm praising You and praying for . . .

CHAPTER 6

Commissioned to Shine and Soar

Jesus came to them and said, "All authority in heaven and on earth has been given to me. Therefore go and make disciples of all nations, baptizing them in the name of the Father and of the Son and of the Holy Spirit, and teaching them to obey everything I have commanded you. And surely I am with you always, to the very end of the age."

MATTHEW 28:18-20

IT'S STILL SURREAL TO think back to the day I walked into a United Nations building to speak to a group of Christians working there. The following week, I walked on stage at a former Broadway theater to give my brief testimony during an evening service at my new home church. I love that both experiences allowed me to encourage people from all over the world.

I'm not one to seek the spotlight, but when God opens a door, I prayerfully go through it. I'm grateful for milestones and breakthrough moments. But whether I'm ministering to one person or hundreds, whether it happens in person or online, and whether I'm near home or far away, it's a privilege and honor to get to speak about the goodness of God and to point others to Christ.

What a long and winding road I've been on to reach this point in my life!

It's one thing to feel God calling you into a certain ministry or path; it's another thing to be released into that season of your life.

Jesus didn't start His public ministry until He was about thirty.

Joshua had to wait forty years in the wilderness before leading the Israelites into the Promised Land.

Twenty-two years passed between Joseph's prophetic dreams that revealed his older brothers would bow down before him and the time they arrived in Egypt looking for grain.

Even David had to wait years for God to fulfill some of His promises to him. He was most likely a teen when the prophet Samuel anointed him as Israel's next king, and he was thirty when he officially started his forty-year reign.

When we consider how long Noah and Abraham and Sarah had to wait, and how many years Mary, the mother of Jesus, must've pondered the prophetic words spoken about her miracle child, we see a pattern:

God isn't in a hurry to fulfill all His dreams for us.

He likes to take His time and prepare us for the promises and dreams He has given us.

No one really explained that to me. I felt all these great calls from God and received some good confirmation from other people, but it was a long and painstaking process until I was living out these callings.

Thankfully, there's beauty and treasure throughout the process, and rewards come when we don't quit.

Nontechie me eventually launched a blog and a YouTube channel, then a website. Then I joined a few other social media platforms to start sharing encouraging words online.

When I won an online devotional-writing contest for a global Christian media outlet, I took that experience as more confirmation that I was on the right track.

After years of angst and frustration and preparation, I entered my season of writing and speaking for God's glory.

I started writing books that have inspired pastors, pastors' wives, chaplains, missionaries, Sunday school teachers, Christian counselors, and those new to the Christian faith. My readers live across the United States and on at least five continents.

Who knew that the niña who was making magazines at home would grow up to write and publish books and devotionals?

God did.

I also started hosting my own book-related events and women's conferences.

I've spoken from pulpits and podiums to various groups that include women and men of diverse backgrounds, ages, and life stages.

I'm one of only a few female instructors at a local Bible school—and the only Latina teacher. Only God could do that!

I'm so grateful that mi familia, including my dear dad, could witness this season of breakthrough.

He and a few others have said I should be a pastor. Only God knows all His plans for me.

This Latina writer, speaker, and audacious dreamer and doer continues to dare to live her God-given dreams.

All glory be to God!

I hope my story inspires you to think about what you could accomplish using your gifts.

My journey hasn't been easy. There have been many moments when I've been tempted to give up. It's felt especially challenging at times as a Latina.

In recent years, I've felt that some people secretly question my nationality and wonder how long I've been in this country and how I got here. Someone once had the gall to give me what felt like an informal citizenship quiz. He asked me easy questions about American culture. I responded with the right clichéd answers. When he asked

me to name America's favorite game, I named a popular board game, and he looked concerned. It seemed as
if somehow my status as an American was in jeopardy
because of my answer. After he clarified that he was looking for a sport, I gave the correct common answer. I guess
I passed his little test and appeared American enough in
his eyes. I had played along, but it bothered me. I wonder
if he questions others upon meeting them.

We can't control what people say or think about us,
but we also don't have to be controlled by their thoughts
or opinions as we live God's divine purpose for us.

I've learned to keep moving forward even when others
aren't supportive.

When I told a pastor I felt God calling me to preach,
he gently corrected me, saying I was being called to *teach*.
I was taken aback. I knew that God wasn't limiting me to
just the classroom. That's when I realized I had never seen
a woman preach on a Sunday in that church—not even
as a guest! This is the case in many church traditions. But
before that moment, I had no idea how controversial the
subject of women preaching could be.

When I was taking an expository preaching class in
Bible school, one of my male classmates remarked how
well I was doing and asked who I was studying with. He
was stunned when I told him I wasn't studying with anyone but the Holy Spirit. It seemed like he couldn't believe

a woman could study the Bible and speak without someone helping her.

When I told a few people I felt God calling me into full-time ministry, they rejoiced at first. But when I started writing and speaking publicly, some ghosted me.

I would eventually be welcomed as a congregant at a new church, but I still didn't quite fit in.

When I asked about jobs at two churches, the only position they offered me was as a receptionist. Given all my work and ministry experience, I wondered why that was the only box they could fit me in. I couldn't help but feel as though there were a secret playbook that said Latinas were perfect for answering a church's phones.

Some people have told me I should write in Spanish. I'd love to have my words translated into different languages, but I've written and spoken in English my entire career. It's as if some Christians don't know what to do with a Latina communicator in the English-speaking world.

I think some people in ministry are surprised that I don't naturally gravitate to Spanish-speaking churches or Spanish-speaking services. That would be an easy box for them to place me in. But we're not created to fit in boxes.

While I appreciate the growing number of Spanish-speaking ministries available, this Latina American feels drawn to multicultural churches and ministries.

No matter our background, we're made to learn and grow alongside a diverse group of people. If everyone we fellowship with and serve with—or every author we read and preacher we listen to—looks and thinks exactly like us, we need to prayerfully allow God to broaden our perspective.

I was disheartened when I started to realize there were cliques in Christian circles. If you didn't go to the same school or belong to the same denomination or pay to be part of someone's group or to attend someone's event, you were basically invisible.

I'm all for vetting people and being wise and discerning about who we serve with, but God doesn't confine us to our own silos or kingdoms.

God chose King David because of his heart and not because of his appearance, his degrees, or the size of his platform.

When I met a ministry leader and told her I was interested in participating in an upcoming event, she immediately suggested I sign up to volunteer. I actually had a little more in mind, but she could see me only as a volunteer. She later got to know me a little better and acknowledged that I had something to say and might make a good panelist or speaker.

When I attended networking events for Christian women, all would be fine until the actual networking time at the end. The women would quickly split up into groups and inevitably start talking with people of their same race or ethnicity. I was usually one of the only Latinas in the room, so I never knew which group to join. When the occasional person approached me, it was usually only to ask if I could take a photo of her group.

I don't mind taking pictures, but when I'm at a networking event for Christian professionals and they'd rather ask me to take a picture than stop and get to know me, that says something.

I don't dwell on those moments.

I appreciate the diverse group of people who have encouraged and prayed for me.

I'm so grateful for doors God continues to open for me.

I'm honored that I can encourage and inspire you to keep going!

People are hurting, and they need us to shine for Jesus.

We must be ready to share with others the hope we have in Christ.

COMMISSIONED TO LIVE YOUR GOD-GIVEN DREAMS

You've prayed, praised, and prepared. You also know your true identity in Christ. You are God's beloved, blessed, and beautiful daughter. You were created with extravagant love, called to honor God, and chosen to bear fruit. You are being conformed to the image of Jesus, and you are clothed with purpose.

Armed with this knowledge, it's time to step out in faith and live your God-given dreams.

The sixth and final truth in the Six Cs of Transformation is that God has commissioned us to shine and soar for His glory.

Jesus proclaimed in Matthew 5:14-16 to His disciples and to us:

> "You are the light of the world. A town built on a hill cannot be hidden. Neither do people light a lamp and put it under a bowl. Instead they put it on its stand, and it gives light to everyone in the house. In the same way, let your light shine before others, that they may see your good deeds and glorify your Father in heaven."

We're called to let our light shine, but not so we're in the spotlight and get all the attention. We're called to shine and to point others to Christ so He gets the glory.

Let's not look at all that we think we're lacking.

God isn't limited by our backgrounds, bank accounts, or résumés. We're more than our nationalities, income levels, or educational achievements. We are who God says we are.

God causes us to flourish and advance and succeed for His name's sake. God will use us as He sees fit and when He deems the time to be right. Let's not forfeit our promises because of the process.

Let's find the joy in our journeys and enjoy today as we prepare for tomorrow.

We're called to live for the applause of the One who truly matters.

We can praise God even before we start seeing the fruit of our labor.

This final chapter is designed to help fuel your faith as you dare to live your God-given dreams.

COMMISSIONED TO MOVE FORWARD WITH GOD

As we dare to live our God-given dreams, we need to stay close to God.

We need to be able to honestly say, "God, if you're not in it, I don't want it."

Moses knew he was nothing without God.

Years ago, one of my choir teachers shared Exodus 33:15-17 with us during rehearsals, and it's stuck with me ever since:

> Moses said to [God], "If your Presence does not
> go with us, do not send us up from here. How
> will anyone know that you are pleased with me

and with your people unless you go with us? What else will distinguish me and your people from all the other people on the face of the earth?"

And the LORD said to Moses, "I will do the very thing you have asked, because I am pleased with you and I know you by name."

What good is it for someone to gain the whole world, yet forfeit their soul?

If we have to lie, steal, cheat, scheme, or compromise to reach our goals, they're not worth it.

Only what we do for God will bless people, communities, and nations for years to come. Since God knows our thoughts, motives, and intentions, let's make sure we continue serving Him with a right heart.

The Bible characters we've read about didn't do their good works for fame and fortune and notoriety. They probably had no idea we'd be talking about them all these years later.

But they left us a legacy of courage and strength and grace and wisdom to learn from.

Now it's our turn.

What legacy would you like to leave?

It's best to pray and seek God before moving ahead with your plans.

If you feel God prompting you to leave behind some things in your past in order to move forward, be encouraged by how the apostle Paul left behind his worldly accolades and accomplishments to follow Christ:

Whatever were gains to me I now consider loss for the sake of Christ. What is more, I consider everything a loss because of the surpassing worth of knowing Christ Jesus my Lord, for whose sake I have lost all things. I consider them garbage, that I may gain Christ and be found in him, not having a righteousness of my own that comes from the law, but that which is through faith in Christ—the righteousness that comes from God on the basis of faith. I want to know Christ—yes, to know the power of his resurrection and participation in his sufferings, becoming like him in his death, and so, somehow, attaining to the resurrection from the dead.

Not that I have already obtained all this, or have already arrived at my goal, but I press on to take hold of that for which Christ Jesus took hold of me. Brothers and sisters, I do not consider myself yet to have taken hold of it.

> But one thing I do: Forgetting what is behind
> and straining toward what is ahead, I press on
> toward the goal to win the prize for which God
> has called me heavenward in Christ Jesus.
>
> PHILIPPIANS 3:7-14

It may not be popular to follow Christ, but let's stay on the narrow path that leads to life and avoid the wide path that leads to ruin. It can be scary to step out in faith, but we can stand on God's Word and grab hold of His promises.

Joshua's story has inspired me tremendously. How did Joshua have the courage to lead the Israelites out of the wilderness and into the Promised Land?

One particular verse helped me as I prepared for my short-term mission trip to Ethiopia.

I thought only "professional" missionaries went to Africa or Asia. I wasn't sure how God could use me in Africa, but He strengthened my heart.

The week before my trip, a woman from my church just "happened" to quote a verse to me. And the day before my flight, I was astonished when my niece and nephew just "happened" to recite the same verse and then gleefully sing me a song based on it: "Have I not commanded you? Be strong and courageous. Do not be afraid;

do not be discouraged, for the LORD your God will be with you wherever you go" (Joshua 1:9).

I felt like I had no business doing outreach or praying for strangers here or abroad.

But when we're filled with Holy Spirit boldness, our fear and timidity fade.

The Holy Spirit leads us to the people we should talk to and prompts us with what to say.

That's how we can talk to strangers, family members, and friends about Jesus.

We need to get out of the way.

It's not about us.

It's all about sharing the love and hope and salvation found in Jesus with a lost and hurting and broken world.

As you consider what God is calling you to do, pray and then act.

Do the research, make the call, send the message, take the class, update your résumé, find a new volunteering opportunity, hire a coach or meet with a mentor, or apply for the job.

Serve God as an accountant, teacher, communicator, entrepreneur, or nurse, or in any other field you feel God calling you to.

Use your compassion for children, the elderly, single moms, or refugees—or your interest in nature, animals, art, music, science, math, or technology—to bring glory to God.

COMMISSIONED DESPITE OPPOSITION

As we talked about in the previous chapter, we're in a spiritual battle. When we step out to live our God-given dreams, we'll encounter opposition. By God's grace, we need to discern who we can trust.

In Matthew 10:16, Jesus warns His disciples and us: "I am sending you out like sheep among wolves. Therefore be as shrewd as snakes and as innocent as doves."

We hopefully won't face imprisonment or death like Jesus' disciples did when they spread the Good News around the ancient world. But we should still be on guard so that we're not deceived or discouraged by those who want to stop us from following God's plan for our lives.

Jesus was followed by crowds, but He chose twelve disciples to learn from Him more closely, and among them was His inner circle of three disciples. We need to be wise about who we let into our inner circles and about who we allow to mentor or counsel us.

Not everyone will approve of your decisions in this new season. Follow God's lead anyway.

People rejected Jesus and His disciples. In Matthew 10:14, we read what Jesus told His disciples to do when people didn't welcome them: "If anyone will not welcome you or listen to your words, leave that home or town and shake the dust off your feet."

Just keep going about your Father's business, as Jesus did.

Jesus faced tremendous opposition, but He never got off track or lost sight of His mission.

We get to continue His divine legacy and tell others about the gospel.

We're the ones shining the light of Christ.

We need to do so with love and respect and gentleness.

Let's be brave and speak the truth in love: "For the Spirit God gave us does not make us timid, but gives us power, love and self-discipline" (2 Timothy 1:7).

Although we're God's beloved daughters, no one is exempt from tests and trials and suffering.

According to 2 Timothy 2:3-7, we're to be like good soldiers, competitive athletes, and hardworking farmers:

> Join with me in suffering, like a good soldier of Christ Jesus. No one serving as a soldier gets entangled in civilian affairs, but rather tries to please his commanding officer. Similarly, anyone who competes as an athlete does not receive the victor's crown except by competing according to the rules. The hardworking farmer should be the first to receive a share of the crops. Reflect on what I am saying, for the Lord will give you insight into all this.

A good soldier endures brutal and demanding training, follows commands, and faithfully serves under harrowing conditions.

A competitive athlete perseveres through years of training and discipline and has the courage and poise to compete under intense pressure.

A hardworking farmer diligently plants seeds by faith and patiently cultivates a crop in all kinds of weather for months before finally receiving the harvest . . . and continues this cycle year after year.

We need much dedication, discipline, patience, fortitude, faith, and prayer as we live our God-given dreams.

We're to run our race with perseverance and with our eyes fixed on Jesus, as we read in Hebrews 12:1-3:

> Since we are surrounded by such a great cloud
> of witnesses, let us throw off everything that
> hinders and the sin that so easily entangles. And
> let us run with perseverance the race marked out
> for us, fixing our eyes on Jesus, the pioneer and
> perfecter of faith. For the joy set before him he
> endured the cross, scorning its shame, and sat
> down at the right hand of the throne of God.
> Consider him who endured such opposition
> from sinners, so that you will not grow weary
> and lose heart.

We must keep running our race, remembering that our ultimate prize is Jesus.

Take a moment to read 2 Corinthians 11:23-33. We may think it's unimaginable how much the apostle Paul suffered for Christ, but we can learn from his example. We'll face different circumstances, but we serve the same God. He got Paul through and taught him that His grace is sufficient.

And Paul learned how to be content despite adversity. While Paul was under house arrest in Rome for serving Jesus, he wrote these words:

> I know what it is to be in need, and I know what it is to have plenty. I have learned the secret of being content in any and every situation, whether well fed or hungry, whether living in plenty or in want. I can do all this through him who gives me strength.
>
> **PHILIPPIANS 4:12-13**

Let's take courage in knowing we can do all that God is calling us to do in His strength.

GLEANING INSIGHT FROM A BIBLE BEAUTY

It was about noon, the hottest time of the day, and a lone Samaritan woman had gone to the well to draw water. She most likely chose that part of the day so she could avoid any crowds and go about her business unnoticed. Perhaps she preferred to stay invisible and isolated instead of having to endure any scornful looks or snickers.

This Samaritan woman must've had a questionable reputation in her town. She had been married five times and was living with a man who wasn't her husband. Perhaps she felt unworthy or unwanted.

This nameless Samaritan woman had no reason to believe this day would be any different from all the others.

But God had His eyes on her, and He was about to commission her to shine and soar for His glory.

In those days, Jews went out of their way to avoid walking through Samaria. They despised and looked down on Samaritans, who were the descendants of Jews who had mixed with Gentiles of various backgrounds.

But the Bible states that Jesus *had* to go through Samaria. He was on a mission. Jesus wasn't afraid to break cultural norms to speak to this Samaritan woman in public. He knew all about her personal life, and He still loved her.

He patiently answered her questions and spoke of the living water that could be found only in Him. He lovingly brought to light her current sins without shaming her.

Jesus had a plan for this unnamed Samaritan woman. He wanted to restore her. After He revealed that He was the long-awaited Messiah, the Samaritan woman felt compelled to go and tell others about Jesus.

God is an expert at using the foolish things of this world to confound the wise.

This unlikely messenger went from being ignored to being an ambassador for Christ. This outcast was chosen to be Jesus' witness and evangelist to the same people who had marginalized and rejected her.

Salvation came to the Samaritan woman's town because of her testimony and her invitation to meet Jesus.

She was no longer defined by her sins but redefined by meeting her Redeemer and sharing her story with others.

What a lasting impact this one woman made! She had more influence than she could ever have imagined, all because of Jesus.

Almighty God *created* and loved the Samaritan woman.

God *called* the Samaritan woman to honor Him.

God *chose* the Samaritan woman to bear fruit.

God *conformed* the Samaritan woman to the image of Christ.

God *clothed* the Samaritan woman with purpose.

God *commissioned* the Samaritan woman to share her testimony and shine and soar for Him.

BELIEVE

A key to answering the call of God on your life and daring to live your God-given dreams is to simply believe! Believe what God has said about Himself in the Bible. Believe what God has said about you. Believe what you feel He has impressed on your heart. And believe that God will see you through any challenge or difficulty you may face.

Let's flex our faith muscles as we go about our Kingdom assignments and wait for our personal breakthroughs, for "without faith it is impossible to please God, because anyone who comes to him must believe that he exists and that he rewards those who earnestly seek him" (Hebrews 11:6).

God loves it when we take Him at His Word. The more we consider the greatness of our God, the more our faith in Him will arise and abound.

If our faith starts to wane, we can always return to some of the following Bible verses to bolster it.

- **When things look impossible:** "Jesus looked at them and said, 'With man this is impossible, but with God all things are possible'" (Matthew 19:26).

- **When we forget Who we're serving:** "Then the word of the LORD came to Jeremiah: 'I am the LORD, the God of all mankind. Is anything too hard for me?'" (Jeremiah 32:26-27).

- **When things look hopeless:** "I know that you can do all things; no purpose of yours can be thwarted" (Job 42:2).

Let's remain at peace knowing that no one and nothing can stop God's purpose for our lives.

God will move heaven and earth to ensure we reach His divine destination for us.

God's promises are yes and amen in Christ.

When God speaks a word to our hearts, we can believe it, for "no word from God will ever fail" (Luke 1:37).

God's power and authority are unlimited.

Let's not put our trust in our personality, platform, paycheck, popularity, or possessions.

Let's put our faith, hope, and confidence where they belong: in Jesus.

Jesus knew His disciples would face many trials, and He knows we will too.

Receive His words of comfort found in John 14:1: "Do not let your hearts be troubled. You believe in God; believe also in me."

Jesus is the answer to our deep questions and longings.

Jesus is the source of our strength.

God never sleeps.

God doesn't lie.

God is trustworthy.

Let's fight the good fight of faith.

May we endure as the apostle Paul did: "I have fought the good fight, I have finished the race, I have kept the faith" (2 Timothy 4:7).

Many times, when I don't understand what's going on or how things will turn out, the Lord gives me these reminders:

- **Be still:** "Be still, and know that I am God; I will be exalted among the nations, I will be exalted in the earth" (Psalm 46:10).

- **Wait:** "Wait for the LORD; be strong and take heart and wait for the LORD" (Psalm 27:14).

- **Believe:** "I remain confident of this: I will see the goodness of the LORD in the land of the living" (Psalm 27:13).

Let's not grow weary before we reap our harvest.

Let's keep on keeping on!

God has a divine timetable. Waiting on God's timing might be hard and frustrating, even painful, but it's worth it.

Beloved, fret not. There's an appointed time for you.

REFLECTING ON BEING COMMISSIONED

I hope you've been drawing strength, courage, and inspiration from the Six Cs of Transformation and from knowing that you are God's beloved, blessed, and beautiful daughter.

Are you ready to dare to live your God-given dreams? You've got what it takes.

With God on our side, we're a force to be reckoned with, as we read in Romans 8:31: "What, then, shall we say in response to these things? If God is for us, who can be against us?"

Let's reflect on what we've been talking about and look at God's plans and thoughts for our futures.

We'll begin by considering the great commission that Jesus gave to His disciples and us:

> Then Jesus came to them and said, "All authority in heaven and on earth has been given to me. Therefore go and make disciples of all nations, baptizing them in the name of the Father and of the Son and of the Holy Spirit, and teaching them to obey everything I have commanded you. And surely I am with you always, to the very end of the age."
>
> MATTHEW 28:18-20

Jesus commissioned His disciples to go into all the world and make disciples and baptize them and teach them to obey all His commands.

He promised to be with them.

They carried out the great commission, and we're the fruit of their labor.

Now God has commissioned *us* to go!

God wants His beloved daughters to go near and far

to share the Good News of Jesus. We can be His compassionate hands and feet, His kind listening ears, and His wise mouthpieces.

We're not called to argue with people or to force them to follow Jesus.

We're called to be His witnesses.

As witnesses, our job is to testify about the goodness of God and the impact Jesus has had on our lives.

There's power in sharing our God stories with others. We don't have to use fancy words or be Bible scholars (unless God calls us to get advanced degrees).

We can be like the man who humbly said that he was once blind—but that Jesus had healed him and now he could see.

God can use you and me.

God designed you. He wants to use your unique background, experience, and personality to reach the people in your community, home, workplace, and school.

You are strategically placed in your family, neighborhood, and industry for this time and season. May you bloom where God has planted you.

Our times are in God's hands.

We are more than conquerors in Christ.

We are overcomers.

We are Christ's ambassadors.

We have good news to share.

Jesus is for all races, backgrounds, cultures, and ethnicities.

The gospel is for whosoever believes.

The Bible talks about how diverse heaven will be. What a lovely picture we see in Revelation 7:9-10:

> After this I looked, and there before me was a great multitude that no one could count, from every nation, tribe, people and language, standing before the throne and before the Lamb. They were wearing white robes and were holding palm branches in their hands. And they cried out in a loud voice:
>
> > "Salvation belongs to our God,
> > who sits on the throne,
> > and to the Lamb."

I'm so grateful for multicultural churches and ministries that reflect the heart of God.

People need the Lord.

Rich, poor, younger, older, women, and men need Jesus.

God has given us spiritual gifts so we can be a blessing inside and outside the church building.

Shine your light wherever God leads you.

Worship God as you're leading a small group or greeting newcomers or pouring coffee or visiting the sick or wherever God has called you to serve.

If God entrusts you with a big platform, remember to honor Him in all you say and do.

We're to honor God with our thoughts, time, talents, and treasures. The end of our earthly lives won't be the end of our story. We know Jesus is preparing a place for His bride.

And Jesus is coming back. The day and hour are unknown.

We have the joy of knowing we'll one day see God in heaven. We'll be asked to give an account of what we did with the gifts He gave us. We're not called to be famous, but to be faithful.

Let's remember the parable of the talents, in which two servants were commended for their faithfulness:

"His master replied, 'Well done, good and
faithful servant! You have been faithful with a few
things; I will put you in charge of many things.
Come and share your master's happiness!'"

MATTHEW 25:21, 23

If you get tired along the way, rest—but don't give up. God will continue to strengthen each of us:

Do you not know?
>   Have you not heard?
The Lord is the everlasting God,
>   the Creator of the ends of the earth.
He will not grow tired or weary,
>   and his understanding no one can fathom.
He gives strength to the weary
>   and increases the power of the weak.
Even youths grow tired and weary,
>   and young men stumble and fall;
but those who hope in the Lord
>   will renew their strength.
They will soar on wings like eagles;
>   they will run and not grow weary,
>   they will walk and not be faint.

ISAIAH 40:28-31

Our faith journey has different stages.

We soar.

We run.

We walk.

For some of us, it will take a lifetime to live out God's call on our lives.

Enjoy the journey.

God is working things together for our good.

God can do immeasurably more than we can dare to even dream.

What's that one audacious dream that's burning in your heart?

God can do even greater things in and through you.

And God is greater than anything we'll ever face.

I don't want to diminish whatever you're going through. But I do want to remind you Who we have in our corner:

> You, dear children, are from God and have
> overcome them, because the one who is in
> you is greater than the one who is in the
> world.
>
> 1 JOHN 4:4

Jesus is the ultimate Counselor, Coach, Confidant, and so much more.

We're never alone. Let's take comfort as we read God's promises in Isaiah 43:2:

> When you pass through the waters,
>   I will be with you;
> and when you pass through the rivers,
>   they will not sweep over you.

When you walk through the fire,
   you will not be burned;
the flames will not set you ablaze.

God won't give up on us. God will finish the good work He started in us.

No matter what we face, let's remember that we win in the end.

Jesus is undefeated, as He assures us in John 16:33:

"I have told you these things, so that in me you may have peace. In this world you will have trouble. But take heart! I have overcome the world."

May you shine for Christ all the days of your life.

REFLECTION QUESTIONS

I hope these questions will help stir your heart. You can use them as journal prompts or as discussion questions with your small group.

1. How do you feel knowing that God placed you where you are for such a time as this?

2. Describe what it would look like for you to soar.

3. How does the story of the Samaritan woman by the well inspire you and demonstrate that almighty God commissioned you to shine and soar?

4. How do you feel knowing that God will be working in you and through you until He calls you home?

5. Are you ready to dream big with God?

6. What is one key takeaway or insight you learned from this chapter?

7. What's one faith step you can prayerfully commit to taking this week to get closer to living your God-given dreams?

ACTION STEP

Take a moment to write down some audacious dreams God has placed in your heart that are immeasurably more than you could ask for or imagine on your own. Write a prayer thanking God in advance for what awaits you here on earth and in heaven.

PRAYER AND PRAISE

Lord, thank You for creating me, calling me, choosing me, conforming me, clothing me, and commissioning me. I'm rejoicing that You love me and have good plans for me. Today, I'm praising You and praying for . . .

Acknowledgments

I'M SO THANKFUL TO GOD for what He has done in and through my life, and how He has allowed me to live so many of the beautiful dreams He placed in my heart.

I'm grateful to the loving parents God gave me, who encouraged me to keep growing as a person and a writer. I'm thrilled that my mom can celebrate this milestone with me. While I would've loved for my dear dad to be here to see this book become a reality, I'm at peace knowing that he is now with our heavenly Father and that I will see him again one day.

I'm grateful to Sue and mi familia's loving support. Thanks for rejoicing with me throughout the years.

Thank you to all my English teachers, journalism professors, and editors who have helped shape me into the writer I am today.

Thank you to my pastors and ministry leaders over the

years who have helped me grow in my faith and become the woman I am today.

Thank you to my friends, who have prayed for and encouraged me during this long journey. May God bless you for your kindness toward me.

Blessings to my past and present students in church and Bible school, as well as my coaching clients. May you continue to grow in your love for Christ, and may your faith continue to arise.

A great big thank you to the awesome teams at NavPress and Tyndale. It was an honor and pleasure to work with you! Thank you for saying yes to this Christian Latina writer from New York and for your dedication to the success of this book. May readers near and far be encouraged and empowered to live their God-given dreams.

NavPress is the book-publishing arm of The Navigators.

Since 1933, The Navigators has helped people around the world bring hope and purpose to others in college campuses, local churches, workplaces, neighborhoods, and hard-to-reach places all over the world, face-to-face and person-by-person in an approach we call Life-to-Life® discipleship. We have committed together to know Christ, make Him known, and help others do the same.*

Would you like to join this adventure of discipleship and disciplemaking?

- Take a Digital Discipleship Journey at **navigators.org/disciplemaking**.
- Get more discipleship and disciplemaking content at **thedisciplemaker.org**.
- Find your next book, Bible, or discipleship resource at **navpress.com**.

 @NavPressPublishing

 @NavPress

 @navpressbooks